PLANT LIFE
A GARDENER'S GUIDE

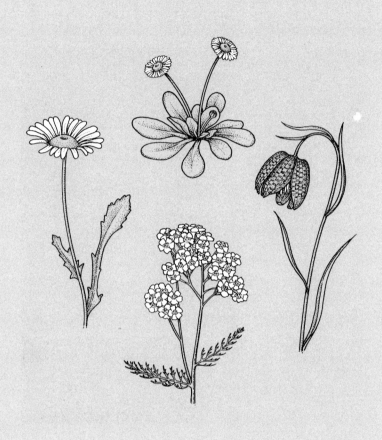

PLANT LIFE
A GARDENER'S GUIDE
SUSAN BERRY AND STEVE BRADLEY

FOREWORD BY JOHN SIMMONS

COLLINS & BROWN IN ASSOCIATION WITH
CHANNEL FOUR TELEVISION CORPORATION

This book has grown out of the television series *Plant Life*, produced by Flashback Television for Channel 4. The authors are most grateful for the help and research of Neil Cleminson, producer and originator, Taylor Downing, executive producer, and David Edgar, director of the series; and also to Ann Bonar for providing the text of 'Growing from Seed'.

First published in Great Britain in 1993 by Collins & Brown Limited, Letts of London House, Great Eastern Wharf, Parkgate Road, London SW11 4NQ

9 8 7 6 5 4 3 2 1

British Library Cataloguing-in-Publication Data:
A catalogue record for this book is available from the British Library.

ISBN 1 85585 176 8 (hardback edition)
ISBN 1 85585 196 2 (paperback edition)

Conceived, edited and designed by
Collins & Brown Limited
Editor: Mandy Greenfield
Art Director: Roger Bristow
Designed by: Nigel Partridge
Filmset by Tradespools Ltd, Frome, Somerset
Reproduction by Scantrans, Singapore
Printed and bound in Italy by New Interlitho SpA, Milan

FRONT JACKET PHOTOGRAPH *A selection of large-flowered hybrid clematis*
BACK JACKET PHOTOGRAPH *A 'Katy' apple tree in full fruit*

HALF TITLE PAGE *Bees visiting sunflowers in order to collect pollen.*
RIGHT *Plants in hot, dry climates, such as these cacti, develop spines to reduce moisture loss.*

CONTENTS

FOREWORD   6

INTRODUCTION
GARDENING WITH NATURE   9

1 THE LIVING SOIL   17

2 THE HIDDEN PLANT   45

3 THE GREEN MACHINE   65

4 GROWING FROM SEED   93

5 THE SENSITIVE PLANT   113

6 SHAPING PLANTS   125

7 THE NATURAL BALANCE   147

GLOSSARY   156

FURTHER READING   157

INDEX   158

ACKNOWLEDGEMENTS   160

PICTURE CREDITS   160

FOREWORD

One of the less appreciated virtues of successful British gardens is that they work with nature, each refining its character according to the landscape, aspect, soils and climate. Subconsciously these gardens express an understanding of the spirit of the organic world, for good gardeners have no difficulty harmonizing their aims with the natural forces of the complex living system that is a garden.

Schoolday botany usually fails to excite its uninterested students or to reveal our relationship with the fascinating, yet vital, world of plants. But often, when the teacher is presented with, say, a pot plant by loving children – reality dawns. How to care for this green and mute living organism? What is the best position for it in the house? What about watering? And this is but the beginning, for although house plants are selected for their tolerance to cultivation and the generally poor environmental conditions provided by the average home, so much more information is needed, if the plant is to prosper.

What then about the proud owner of a new house that comes with its plot of ground? Making a garden! Good garden-makers often have intuitive skills, but all gardeners can gain from understanding the biology of plants. Complex though they are, living systems are not hard to understand, especially if clearly and interestingly revealed – the art of good television and journalism.

Many people do not realize that plants have hormones and circulation systems, which are responsive to their environment. The use of time-lapse photography and filming across the seasons of the year allows these and other changes and developments to be seen more easily. Making plant science accessible is the aim of the television series that accompanies this volume.

What then are we doing in creating a garden? A very difficult question to answer. In nature, each habitat evolves as a complex of the natural resources available to its flora and fauna. It is successional, ever-changing in season and time.

But the idealized natural world is ruthlessly competitive. All living creatures have a great natural drive for survival. It is a war, with each developing the means to increase and maximize its kind. There are strategies for suppression: consider the sycamore's mat of autumn leaves, killing the grass beneath it and recycling its annual shedding. Chemical warfare, too, as roots put out exudates that can suppress the growth of other plants – weeds grow best on bare earth. There is a continuing battle for light, water and mineral resources that goes largely unnoticed.

Enter the gardener. Have you thought what you are doing when you are weeding? Suppressing the competition of some plants in favour of your chosen ones. Or mowing? A mechanical grazing system that favours grasses. By all the methods available to the gardener it is possible to maintain a greater species richness and infinite aesthetic associations that go beyond nature's intent – plants from many different habitats in a managed system.

Good gardening means being alive to the web of life. A garden's soil contains millions of creatures and many microscopic fungi and bacteria that associate with plant roots. Chalk soils are rather impoverished, free-drained, alkaline, though sometimes with an acid turf surface, and provide a habitat for many specialized plants. So when a clematis, which grows naturally in such soil, succumbs in a cold, wet garden clay, it should not be a surprise. Similarly, we might well expect a Japanese woodland maple to shrivel in the open in a hot, dry sandy soil.

Some plants are more tolerant, gardeners' friends. The bistort (*Polygonum bistorta*) of moist meadows will tolerate much drier conditions. And pruning too. Magnolias' wounds heal slowly, but apples produce a natural wound-healing substance – and we select. As in hedge-cutting, we choose woody plants that are tolerant of cutting and produce many axillary shoots after the terminal buds are removed from them. Just as we select suitable materials for walls, so are hedge plants (living walls) carefully selected.

Plants have their rhythms. Every year the sequence and abundance of flowering varies from species to species, according to the habitat in which each originally evolved. Seeds similarly need specific temperature patterns to trigger germination. Holly (*Ilex aquifolium*) seed, for example, germinates better if it has a warm (ripening) period before a cold (winter) sequence, and the warmth of (spring) sowing.

Why is it then that we can gain such fulfilment from creating a garden and making plants grow? From the eye, through the brain, to the hand goes a process of creation – observing, understanding, adapting, creating. The pleasure of this creation: evening sun, low and vividly colouring the sky, swifts dive and squeal overhead, the first bats quarter their territory, the fruits surround; of orchard and border, of labour and knowledge – and from knowledge comes the love of gardens. Perhaps, too, the answer to my earlier question.

I hope that this book and its accompanying series offer reader and viewer alike a key to a greater share of this enjoyment.

JOHN B.E. SIMMONS, OBE, VMH
CURATOR, ROYAL BOTANIC GARDENS, KEW
JUNE 1993

GARDENING WITH NATURE

It is easier to do something out of habit than it is to consider why you are doing it. As small children, we often learn by observing how other people do things, subconsciously copying them later. Many of us learned about gardening by watching our parents or grandparents and, without thinking, we tend to do as they did. If they went around the garden in February, pruning the shrubs, we tend to assume that is what we must do, without ever questioning it.

Gardeners who forget their debt to nature do so at their peril. Small areas of the garden can be turned over to native plants, such as cowslips and bluebells (LEFT), and frogs and toads (BELOW) will spawn happily in small pools.

Gardening knowledge is often a strange amalgam of observation, experience and hearsay, with little real understanding of how or why certain tasks are performed. Because gardening is, for most of us, a hobby, we do not give it the kind of detailed attention that we might give to our work, for example.

Would-be gardeners divide as a result into two camps: those who think there is nothing to it – any fool can look after a garden – and those who are convinced that it is hedged about with mystique. In fact, being a good gardener (and that is not the same as being a good garden designer, which requires entirely different skills) is mainly a matter of applied common sense and experience. It is no accident that today many of the most successful gardeners are women, since raising children and plants call for many of the same qualities: an ability to observe closely, think for yourself and learn from your mistakes.

One of the inherent difficulties of gardening is that the gardener has a curiously schizoid relationship with nature. But he or she will only succeed by working with nature rather than against it – the key to success lies in harnessing nature's forces to work to your own advantage. This presupposes some understanding of how nature operates.

Plant Life: A Gardener's Guide attempts to explain just that, by describing the cycle of plant growth, development and decay. Although much fun has been made of people (including royalty!) who talk to plants, the sensitivity of plants should not be underestimated, since they do respond to both sound and light waves. They are, after all, living organisms, and failure to understand that they – like people – have particular needs will spell disaster for the gardener.

Perhaps the first lesson for any gardener to learn is to respect the power of nature, and to try to understand the finely tuned balancing act that most plants perform in order to stay alive. Gardeners who interfere insensitively with nature do so at their peril.

Take, for example, our attempts to grow food crops on a small area of soil. We force the plants to produce fruit, or tubers, or seeds for us, tearing them out to harvest them when it suits our needs, not the plant's. The natural cycle of growth and decay is interrupted, with the result that no nitrogen is returned to the soil to provide the basic food for next year's crops. Failure by us to provide nitrogen will result in a poorer crop next year, and continual interruption of the natural cycle – without replacing what we have taken out – will lead in the end to the production of no crops at all.

Another example of our inability to understand nature's purpose is shown in our desire to grow plants that we have seen in catalogues, regardless of whether they are suited to the conditions we are going to offer them. We decide, perhaps, that we like plants with enormous scarlet flowers, and rush down to the garden centre to purchase these objects of desire, only to find that they promptly shrivel and die in our gardens. The reason lies in the fact that these wonderful plants with exotic flowers may have have evolved over thousands of years in climates very different from our own – perhaps in a hot, desert environment, with sandy soil and very little rainfall. Transposed into a garden on clay soil, in mid-Wales, with high quantities of rainfall each year, the plant will simply rot away.

Understanding what you can offer the plant, in terms of your own garden's climate, soil conditions and aspect, is a vital part of successful gardening. Instead of working from the standpoint of what you would like to grow, you are far better off trying to analyse what you can actually provide. How much time do you have to devote to the garden? If you have a great deal of time, you can opt for the more unusual, non-native plants, because you will be able to provide the conditions that they require – protecting them in winter, feeding them regularly, watering when necessary. If, like many busy people today, you want a garden but have only a limited amount of time to devote to it, then you need to adopt a rather different approach.

Many of us are slaves to fashion without really thinking about the consequences. Gardening itself has been the subject of changing fashions since the concept of the pleasure garden was first introduced (see page 13), but for many of us today ecological concerns have become increasingly important, and to some extent garden styles and designs now take this into account.

CHEMICALS – FOR OR AGAINST?

In the last 10 years the emphasis has shifted away from the use of chemicals in the garden, as realization has dawned that over-dependence on chemicals is ruining our environment. Although we often feel powerless to halt the erosion of the Earth's diminishing natural resources, we can at least, in our gardens, behave in an environmentally conscious way, without becoming martyrs to the concept. You do not need to be an expert on the latest developments in biological control to run a well-balanced garden. Making compost – recycling garden waste – makes sense. So does using our knowledge about the way plants grow to avoid causing diseases, which then have to be eradicated using chemicals. Just as a course of antibiotics to treat disease in humans destroys many of the benevolent bacteria that live in the gut, causing secondary problems such as fungal disease, so reaching for the chemical cupboard to solve a problem in the garden brings in its wake a chain of reactions. If chemical pesticides are to be used, they should be considered as the last resort, never the first line of attack. Excessive use of fertilizers, for example, to try to create larger crops creates overly lush leaf growth, which is more likely to fall prey to pests and diseases. It is far better to try to avoid the problems in the first place, by growing plants that are adapted to the environment, which are naturally healthier and less likely to succumb to disease as a result.

A Helping Hand from Nature

One of the most enjoyable aspects of gardening occurs when nature decides to offer a helping hand rather than – as often seems to be the case – frustrate your well-laid plans. Plants self-seeding in cracks between paving-stones, producing replicas of some of your best-loved plants, such as lady's mantle (*Alchemilla mollis*), anchusa (*Anchusa* sp.), mullein (*Verbascum* sp.), poppy (*Papaver* sp.) and love-in-a-mist (*Nigella damascena*), help to make up for the endless war that you wage on the weed-seeds that are hell-bent on doing the same.

Devices such as black plastic, covered with a layer of bark chippings, suppress weeds well, while doing no damage to the environment (unlike herbicides), and also cut down on the work in the garden.

Enriching the soil with plenty of organic matter from your own compost heap – so encouraging the worm population to multiply and work for you, as well as giving the plants a better chance of becoming tough and healthy – clearly makes good gardening sense. One of the greatest rewards of gardening is that you get back, by and large, what you put in: 'As ye sow, so shall ye reap.'

Nature has devised some curious and fascinating ways of helping plants to overcome the hazards of the environment in which they find themselves – their leaves may have enlarged to cope with shade, or become felted to cope with water loss; their spines may have grown long and sharp to deter predators and conserve moisture; their flowers may have become large and colourful to attract pollinating insects. Some of these adaptations seem to belong more to the world of science fiction than to botany, particularly when you notice the complicated reactions of some plants to having their leaves touched, or the way an insectivorous plant can quickly catch and trap its insect prey.

For town-dwellers, gardening offers a much-needed opportunity to observe some of the basic rules of nature at work. Even in a small London plot, you can do your bit for the local wildlife population. A friend has a large cherry tree in a north London garden. The tree is not particularly handsome, and the fruit is neither large nor sweet, but it is plentiful. Unfortunately, the tree has not been pruned and most of the cherries are a good 12m (40ft) up from the ground, so that only a performing acrobat could harvest them. The birds, however, have no such problem. Each June the tree attracts an incredible array of birds, including the usual riff-raff of sparrows, pigeons and starlings. This annual beanfeast for birds seems well worth laying on at the expense of growing a more elegant, but less beneficial, ornamental shrub.

ABOVE AND RIGHT *Wild plants will proliferate and seed themselves, one particular plant often dominating the others, as these oxeye daisies and cowslips demonstrate.*

CHANGING FASHIONS IN GARDENING

The natural approach to gardening has been in and out of fashion in different eras. In the seventeenth century, when man was trying to demonstrate his new-found control of the environment, everything in the garden looked artificial. Plants were clipped and shaped into contorted forms; water was channelled into canals; long, straight avenues of trees were planted. Everywhere man's hand could be seen, controlling, organizing and taming nature.

By the early eighteenth century, a total transformation had been wreaked on gardens. Capability Brown and Humphry Repton, in the age of Romanticism, advocated a return to nature, and gardens became elaborately wrought copies of the natural landscape. Rivers were dammed to make lakes, hills and valleys were created, and knots of trees planted to echo the natural outlines of the landscape beyond the garden. Flowers were no longer fashionable and were relegated to the kitchen garden. In their place came great sweeps of grass.

In time, this natural landscape gave way to the stiff, structured approach of the Victorian garden, where gardeners vied with one another to include exotic ways of incorporating the vast range of plants being brought back from all parts of the world by plant-hunters. Great glass conservatories were built to house these collections, and large formal borders and symmetrically planted bedding were the order of the day until William Robinson, in the late nineteenth century, started to advocate, once again, a return to nature in his seminal book *The Wild Garden*.

The aftermath of the First World War saw a lack of manpower to maintain the large gardens, and gardening became much more the responsibility of the woman of the house, with a greater concentration on flowers and flower borders, thanks in part to the influence of Gertrude Jekyll, an enthusiastic advocate of the English flower border.

In the last couple of decades we have seen another resurgence of interest in natural gardening and a growing desire to find less environmentally harmful ways of controlling nature. Organically grown produce has become more available and gardeners increasingly express concern about the use of chemicals.

A small pond (see page 15) is another great draw for wildlife, encouraging insects for the birds to feed on, frogs and newts. And a small wild patch at the end of a suburban garden (see page 14) can provide valued cover for insects, as well as nectar for bees and butterflies.

NATURAL HABITATS

These days there are few great wilderness areas left untouched by tourism or commercial exploitation, and in Britain there are singularly few. One area deliberately left untouched, however, lies not in the highlands of Scotland or Wales, as you might expect, but in Hertfordshire. At the Rothamstead experimental station, established in 1843 by chemists John Laws and Henry Gilbert, a century-old experiment is being conducted into the use of organic and inorganic fertilizers. In one area scientists have left a plot, previously planted with cereals, to the ravages of nature. Over the years, what was once an arable field has turned itself into a deciduous tree forest of oak (*Quercus* sp.), sycamore (*Acer pseudoplatanus*) and ash (*Fraxinus* sp.). Even the shrub layer of hawthorn (*Crataegus* sp.) that sprung up is being forced out by lack of light, and the ground is covered by ivy (*Hedera* sp.) in areas of dense shade and by dog's mercury (*Mercurialis perennis*), violets (*Viola* sp.) and the occasional arum lily (*Arum maculatum*) in areas of light shade.

CREATING A WILD-FLOWER MEADOW

One of the most pleasing ways of attracting wildlife to the garden is by creating a wild-flower meadow. The term 'meadow' is rather a misnomer, since it implies something very large: the old-fashioned 'flowery mead' is perhaps a better description, since you can, in fact, create just such a wild-flower sanctuary on a suburban plot. Various wild-flower meadows in Britain have now been preserved by charitable organizations, including Marden Meadow, which is looked after by the Kent Trust for Nature organization. One of perhaps four or five such meadows in Britain, it contains a rich selection of wild flowers, including the rare green-winged orchid (*Orchis morio*).

Although it may not be possible for you to create such a distinctive preserve, a whole range of attractive native flowers can be persuaded to grow in ordinary gardens, if given the correct treatment. Buttercups (*Ranunculus acris*), oxeye daisies (*Leucanthemum vulgare*), bugle (*Ajuga* sp.), rattle (*Pedicularis palustris*), clover (*Trifolium* sp.) and fine grasses will all grow fairly easily, attracting a host of butterflies and insects.

WILD-FLOWER MIXTURE FOR A MEADOW

Aim to include at least some of the following in your wild-flower meadow:
Common mallow (*Malva sylvestris*)
Cuckoo flower (*Cardamine pratensis*)
Dandelion (*Taxacum officinale*)

Yarrow

Oxeye daisy

Field daisy

Dyer's-greenweed (*Genista tinctoria*)
Feverfew (*Chrysanthemum parthenium*)

Field daisy (*Bellis perennis*)
Germander speedwell (*Veronica chamaedrys*)
Lady's bedstraw (*Galium verum*)
Lesser trefoil (*Trifolium dubium*)
Meadow buttercup (*Ranunculus acris*)
Meadow cranesbill (*Geranium pratense*)

Snake's head fritillary

Oxeye daisy (*Leucanthemum vulgare*)
Snake's head fritillary (*Fritillaria meleagris*)
Yarrow (*Achillea millefolium*)

GRASSES CONTAINED IN WILD-FLOWER SEED MIXTURES

Cocksfoot (*Dactyllis glomerata*)

Common bent (*Agrostis tenuis*)

Common quaking-grass (*Briza media*)

Crested dog's-tail (*Cynosurus cristatus*)

Meadow fescue (*Festuca pratensis*)

Meadow foxtail (*Alopecurus pratensis*)

Perennial rye-grass (*Lolium perenne*)

Red fescue (*Festuca rubra*)

Smooth meadow-grass (*Poa pratensis*)

Soft-brome (*Bromus mollis*)

Sweet vernal-grass (*Anthoxanthum odoratum*)

Tufted hair-grass (*Deschampsia caespitosa*)

Yellow oat-grass (*Trisetum flavescens*)

Yorkshire-fog (*Holcus lanatus*)

To create such a meadow in a garden you first have to get rid of any perennial weeds, particularly creeping thistles (*Cirsium arvense*), which tend to dominate other species. Then sow the wild-flower mix. Simply because the meadow contains wild flowers does not mean, however, that you can then ignore it. It should be given a hay-cut (in other words, leave about 7–8cm/3in of grass and flowers) in July in its second year, and again in September. No fertilizer should be added, since the lack of nutrients encourages the more delicate wild flowers at the expense of the more rampant thistles and perennial weeds.

MAKING A POND

One of the best materials for a making garden pond is heavy-duty butyl liner, which easily takes the shape of the hole that you dig for the pond. If your aim is to attract wildlife, make sure that at least one of the pond's edges is shallow, allowing small creatures and birds to drink from the water. A shallow rim is also useful if you want to grow marginal plants, which will provide cover and shelter for wildlife that is using the pond.

RIGHT *Dig out an appropriately sized hole for the pond and remove any sharp stones that might puncture the lining. Lay the butyl liner, which must be large enough to allow a 15cm (6in) margin around the edge of the pond. Weight the margins temporarily with stones, and finish with whatever material suits your garden style.*

THE LIVING SOIL

S ome 450 million years ago, plants first spread out over the land. As slow colonization progressed, an interaction began between the underlying rock and the remains of the plants. Soil, in all its various forms, was gradually being produced and eventually became the land form upon which all life on Earth ultimately depends.

The ability of animals to move allows them freedom to choose the most favourable habitats, under changing conditions. A plant, on the other hand, is usually in one place for life, its root system hidden, its destiny dependent on the soil for anchorage, nutrients and moisture.

Plants have adapted over the years to different climates and soil conditions. On chalk downland (LEFT) you find a range of chalk-loving plants, including orchids and wild thyme. Thymus praecox articus (BELOW), a small creeping thyme, also does best in chalky soil.

Plants are highly resilient and can survive in very marginal conditions, actually growing out of rock and even brickwork, and certainly capable of living in very poor soil. Many plants do not even grow in a soil environment – all they need is a source of moisture, nutrients and some support. Some plants grow on other plants – these are known as epiphytes – and are usually found high up in trees in tropical rain forests.

The important thing to remember about your own garden is that you are pretty much stuck with whatever you have in the way of garden soil. You cannot completely dig it out and replace it, so you must get to know it, if you are to cultivate it successfully. You need to understand its texture, and whether it consists of heavy clay or a light sandy soil; and you need to find out its pH (potential of hydrogen) in order to ascertain how acidic, or how alkaline, it is (see page 29). Then you are in a position to choose the plant material that is most suited to that environment.

Different kinds of soil are found in the different regions of the world. Take one area in Britain, for example, such as a valley in Upper Teesdale, where at one time glacial ice scoured the valley, eating away at the rock. Nowadays, the river continues the work of inexorable erosion. The ground-down particles of rock form the underlying basis of the soil there, to which organic elements are added from the decomposed remains of plants and animals.

In a country like Britain, which has been cultivated for thousands of years, the soil is made up not only of the underlying geological strata, but also of the product of years of farming. As a result, the soils in Britain are many and various. Clays, sands and loams all give colour and texture to the patchwork of fields once typical of the British countryside.

In the Fenlands, for instance, deep, dark, heavy soils are particularly good at supporting crops such as sugar beet and potatoes. The dead organic remains from the rushes and sedges that grow naturally in these damp, low-lying lands retain the moisture and ensure a good soil structure. Other edible crops prefer lighter, more free-draining soils with rather higher levels of mineral nutrients. The chalk downlands of Wiltshire, for example, suit the herbage grasses and their larger cousins, the cereal crops.

In our gardens, soils are even more varied than those under the plough. Most of them are able to support a colourful range of handsome plants, and even those from the most remote and exotic parts of the world seem to find an agreeable root-hold in Britain's temperate climate. However, in order to grow a wide range of healthy plants, you need to know what your soil is composed of, and – if necessary – how to improve it.

SOIL STRUCTURE

Although to the uninitiated soil looks pretty much like – well, soil, from the gardener's point of view it is well worth knowing a bit about soil's actual composition. Correct analysis of the soil is one of the key elements in the success – or otherwise – of growing certain types of plants, and the kind of soil you have in your garden will (together with other factors such as climate and rainfall) determine which particular plants you can grow in it.

Since the soil is made up of mineral particles to which organic matter has been added, different kinds of soil clearly depend on the nature of the underlying rock and whether you live in a river valley, where those particles have been ground down to form silt or clay, or in areas with only a thin covering of soil, where it may well be chalky or sandy. These underlying conditions also determine how acid or alkaline the soil is (see page 27), another important factor in determining what can be grown in it.

IMPROVING SOIL STRUCTURE

Although nature can cope perfectly well with poor soil conditions, ensuring that only suitable plants will survive to propagate themselves, the gardener wants a far wider scope. To grow a larger range of plants than nature had in mind, it is therefore important to improve the soil in various ways.

TESTING YOUR SOIL
Dig up a trowelful of soil from your garden and squeeze it between your fingers to find out its basic structural properties. Clay soil feels sticky when rubbed between your fingers, and has an almost plasticine-like quality. Sand feels very gritty, and the particles in it are clearly visible. Silty soil is neither excessively sticky nor very grainy.

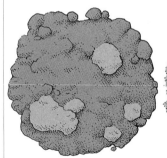

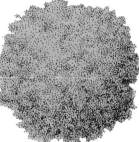

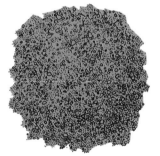

CLAY
This has the finest particles of minerals, and the least amount of air in its structure. Unless you work lots of grit and organic matter into it, it will be hard to grow a good range of plants on clay.

SILT
The particles in silt lie somewhere between those of sand and clay soils in size and, provided it contains lots of organic matter, silt makes good garden soil. It has a silky feel and is often found in river valleys.

SAND
This has the coarsest particles of minerals, and although it is well aerated, water runs through it very easily. Again, it needs lots of organic matter added to it, to bind the particles and improve its moisture-retaining properties.

LOAM
This is the soil structure for which all gardeners aim: a good combination of organic matter with the basic mineral particles, whether sand, silt or clay. It is achieved by generous and regular applications of composted material.

Plants will not thrive unless they have a certain amount of oxygen for their roots, and heavy clay soil has such small particles that very little air penetrates it. In such circumstances, it is the gardener's job to create a more porous texture to the soil, normally by adding lots of organic matter, and possibly some grit. Another way of improving heavy clay soil is to add lime to it (see page 27). And if the soil is very heavily waterlogged and fails to drain well, you may have to consider creating some form of artificial drainage as well (see page 22).

With light sandy soil, the main problem is that it drains too freely, retaining very little moisture. In periods of drought, therefore, plants will suffer and possibly die. Again, the answer is to add plenty of bulky organic matter to help to bind the particles together.

To find out what your soil consists of, you need to take a lump of it in your hand and crumble it between your fingers. If the soil is very sandy, you will actually hear the sound of the grains rubbing together, and you can feel them between your fingers. A less sandy soil, often found in areas surrounding a river bed, is silt, which has a soapy feel to it. The third kind of soil – clay – is very heavy and sticky, with a glaze on its surface that causes it almost to shine.

These are the basic soil types that you will find in your garden. What you have to try to do is create what is known as loam, which is a mixture of any of these types with organic matter. A good loamy soil feels light and friable to the touch, and has a pleasant, brown, earthy colour to it. This is the kind of soil that encourages earthworm activity (see page 33), is well aerated, because it is neither too dense nor too crumbly, and holds moisture to the right degree for plant health and vigour.

SOIL PROBLEMS

We are encouraged to think that digging is important, and indeed it is vital to introduce plenty of organic matter into an otherwise starved soil. But soil disturbance can cause real problems for gardeners, who

SOIL POLLUTION

The various chemicals emitted from a variety of industries and from car exhausts are eventually washed back into the soil through rainfall. In some areas, the large quantities of sulphur dioxide and nitrogen oxide contained in acid rain have become extremely damaging to plants.

Plants simply cannot cope with such high levels of acidity, because they cannot draw the nutrients they need from the soil in these conditions. Where the soil is naturally alkaline, the effect is less damaging, but where acid rain falls on already acid soil, the impact is doubled. And when the acid from the soil, combined with the acid in the rainfall, gets into water courses, it will start to kill off fish and aquatic plants.

In some areas, liming the soil (see page 27) helps to counteract the process. In parts of the Lake District, for instance, where sheep farming is a major industry, the soil is regularly limed in order to improve grass production, which otherwise slows down in overly acid conditions.

ABOVE *Raised beds can be useful for creating special planting schemes. If your own soil is chalky, and you want to grow acid-loving plants such as azaleas and pieris, you can fill a raised bed with a suitably acid growing medium, as here. Alternatively, in a garden recently created from a building site, a small raised bed with imported topsoil gives you the chance to grow some interesting plants, while working on the soil elsewhere in the garden to improve it.*

are often unaware of its effects. Normally, the benefits of adding plenty of organic matter and aerating the soil outweigh the problems created by the disturbance, but each time the soil is turned over, it gives the insects and bacteria living there an unpleasant shock, so that instead of quietly carrying on chewing, they have to find new routes and tunnels, since the digging has blocked or broken down the old ones. When you think of the stress of moving house, you begin to appreciate what you are doing to the insect and bacteria population of your soil!

One of the major problems for anyone gardening on a new plot is not just the type of soil but what has happened to it in the past. The heavy machinery used in house building can create havoc with the soil, because it squashes it (particularly if it is heavy clay anyway) into a dense, airless mass into which roots cannot penetrate. Sometimes the soil compaction lies some distance below the surface, but it acts like a paving slab, preventing roots from growing through it and making earthworm activity much less likely to occur. Without improvement to its structure, no plant would survive in this kind of soil. If you are faced with soil that has been badly compressed, your only recourse is to break through this layer by digging, adding as much well-rotted compost as you can, and possibly grit as well, to improve aeration. Even fairly lightweight machinery can compact the soil; so, too, can

CREATING A SOAKAWAY

If the soil in your garden comprises very heavy clay, and refuses to drain properly, you will probably need to put in some form of drainage. The simplest method is to create a soakaway – in other words, to provide a drain, or drains, that run away at an angle into a pit filled with rubble, so that water does not pool on the surface of the soil. On an allotment or in a vegetable garden you can simply create a series of ditches, but in an ornamental garden, where you do not wish the mechanics of the drainage to be visible, you will need to bury a drainage pipe to collect the excess water. Remember to lay the pipe at a slight angle.

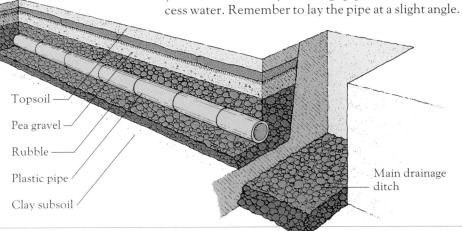

RIGHT *Bury the drainage pipe, or pipes, about 45cm (18in) deep, running at a slight slope from the area to be drained to the sides of the garden, where you should construct a deeper pit filled with rubble, through which the water can dissipate.*

Topsoil

Pea gravel

Rubble

Plastic pipe

Clay subsoil

Main drainage ditch

the gardener, by tramping up and down over newly dug soil. One of the reasons that many gardening books recommend that you put planks down when you are working on a vegetable plot, for example, is so that you do not tread down the soil so hard that no air penetrates. It is also essential to avoid working in very wet conditions, as this may cause damage to the soil structure.

WATERLOGGED SOIL

One of the common soil problems that gardeners have to deal with is waterlogging – when more water enters the soil than drains out of it. Most plant roots are unable to function effectively in waterlogged soil and will simply rot away if drainage is not provided. You can test whether your garden is not draining properly by digging a large hole and chucking in a couple of buckets of water. If the water does not drain away within a few hours, the soil is probably fairly heavy clay and needs artificial drainage, as well as a long-term programme of added organic matter. Where there is a waterlogging problem you have two options. You can either create a bog garden (see page 23) for plants that thrive in these conditions, or you can drain the soil artificially. There are various ways of doing the latter. The easiest is to contour the garden slightly and create series of ditches, so that the surplus water flows away from the site. Underground drains may be needed in an ornamental garden (see above), draining to a soakaway.

PLANTING WITH NATURE

If your soil presents specific problems to do with its structure – being wet or very dry, for example – then rather than expend great quantities of energy trying to bring it closer to the norm, you can always copy nature, and grow those plants that would thrive naturally in such conditions.

For instance, if you have an area of poorly draining land in your garden, often as the result of a very clay soil, you have the ideal conditions in which to create a bog garden. The virtues of a bog garden are that the plants that thrive in these conditions are usually large and lush, with beautiful foliage – *Rodgersia*, *Peltiphyllum* and *Zantedeschia*, for example. So before you drain the site, think about whether it might be worth while adapting to the conditions that you have – rather than the reverse – and growing what nature intended for it.

If you want to grow bog plants, but do not have the necessary waterlogged soil, you can simulate the conditions by installing a waterproof liner, in a gentle bowl shape, at a depth of half a metre (1–2ft) below the surface, or by sinking a few flowerpots in close proximity in one area of the garden (see below).

If the land is not naturally damp, you will have to water frequently in dry weather. One of the best ways of doing this is by laying a rubber pipe, with perforations in it, along the top of the liner when you make

MAKING A SMALL BOG GARDEN

If you want to grow only one or two moisture-loving plants, a simple solution is to use a large clay pot or half-barrel (line the latter with butyl liner or black plastic) and fill it with soil to which plenty of organic matter has been added. A good plant for this would be *Zantedeschia aethiopica* 'Crowborough', with its handsome white spathes, or one of the ligularias, such as *Ligularia dentata* 'Desdemona' or *L. stenocephala* 'The Rocket', as they enjoy damp, rich soil. The pot must have drainage holes in the bottom.

RIGHT *A wooden barrel with a depth of about 75cm (2½ft) makes an ideal container for one of the larger moisture-loving plants. A few bits of broken pot in the base over the drainage holes will prevent these from clogging up with soil.*

the bog garden. Allow the open end of the pipe to rest just above the soil surface some distance away.

When you wish to water the bog garden, it is quite simple to do so through the exposed pipe using a hose. The end of the pipe can easily be disguised with planting. This method of watering ensures that the water gets to the roots of the plants rather than simply lying on the top layer of the soil.

PLANTS FOR DAMP GROUND

Brunnera macrophylla
Cardiocrinum giganteum
Gunnera manicata
Heracleum
   mantegazzianum
Hosta fortunei
H. sieboldiana 'Elegans'
H. ventricosa
Ligularia dentata
   'Desdemona'
L. stenocephala
   'The Rocket'
Lysichitum americanum
Peltiphyllum peltatum
Petasites japonicus
Rheum palmatum
Rodgersia pinnata
R. tabularis
Zantedeschia aethiopica

LEFT *The water gardens at Wisley in spring, with a display of moisture-loving plants, including candelabra primulas in flower in the foreground and Japanese irises behind them.*

ABOVE *Shade varies from the deepest obscurity of a coniferous forest, where very little grows underneath the light-excluding canopy of trees, to the dappled light of deciduous woodland, where foxgloves (Digitalis sp.) and aquilegias, among others, enjoy the cool, partial shade.*

RIGHT *The sun rose,* Cistus × purpureus, *as its name implies, enjoys the benefit of a really warm, sunny situation. Many of the sun-loving plants that we grow in our gardens come from the Mediterranean regions and are not truly frost-hardy.*

PLANTS FOR DRY SHADY AREAS

Very dry areas of the garden can also be used to grow interesting plants that have adapted to these conditions in nature. The principal factor is going to be whether the dry area is in full sun or partial shade, since very different genera thrive under these different conditions. According to Beth Chatto, an expert on finding the right place for the right plant, those that thrive well in dry shade include the following:

Ajuga	Lamium maculatum
Alchemilla	Melissa
Arum	Polygonatum
Bergenia	Pulmonaria
Brunnera	Symphytum
Digitalis	Tellima
Epimedium	Teucrium
Euphorbia robbiae	Thalictrum
Geranium macrorrhizum	Tiarella
Hedera	Vinca
Helleborus foetidus	Viola labradorica
Iris foetidissima	Waldsteinia

PLANTS FOR DRY SUNNY AREAS

Plants that like dry sun include Mediterranean ones, such as many of the more tender herbs. Plants for dry sunny conditions often have small, hairy or felted leaves to help to conserve moisture and include:

Achillea	Some euphorbias, such
Allium (some)	as E. polychroma and
Anthemis tinctoria	E. wulfenii
Artemisia	Foeniculum
Asphodeline	Gaura
Ballota	Gladiolus
Calamintha	Lavandula
Cistus (below)	Leucanthemum
Crinum	Linaria
Dianthus	Linum
Diascia	Onopordum
	Penstemon
	Perovskia
	Phlomis
	Ruta graveolens
	Salvia
	Santolina
	Sedum
	Sempervivum
	Senecio
	Stachys
	Thymus
	Verbascum

PLANTS FOR CLAY SOILS

Gardeners are always moaning about clay, and how difficult it is to grow anything on it. Margery Fish wrote an excellent book on the subject, *Gardening on Clay & Lime*, and Beth Chatto, who has a hefty streak of clay in her garden in Essex, provides lists in her catalogue of plants that do well on clay:

Acanthus	Petasites
Alchemilla	Polygonatum
Aruncus	Primula (some)
Bergenia	Prunella
Caltha	Rheum
Campanula × burghaltii	Rodgersia
C. persificolia	Rubus
Epimedium	Salix
Euphorbia robbiae	Symphoricarpos
Gentiana acaulis	Symphytum
Geranium	Trachystemon
Hacquetia	Vinca (below)
Hedera	
Helleborus	
Hemerocallis	
Hosta	
Inula	
Lamiastrum	
Levisticum	
Liriope muscari	
Lonicera	
Peltiphyllum	

According to Margery Fish, it is perfectly possible to have a beautiful garden on clay soil, but you have to abide by certain rules. First of all, she advised, do not walk on it when it is wet, because it compacts the soil even further. It helps if you keep beds narrow, plant in blocks rather than in rows, with numerous paths, and use a plank to walk on.

Margery also suggested digging no deeper than 30cm (12in), because the clay gets very sticky, and she recommended using mulches and ground-cover plants to keep the moisture in the soil, since when clay does dry out, it turns into a desert. Another valuable tip is to use plenty of coarse sand in the planting hole every time a new plant is put in.

GRASSES FOR CLAY SOILS

Alopecurus pratensis 'Aureus'	Miscanthus
	Molinia
Arundinaria (bamboo)	Panicum
Carex	Sasa veitchii (bamboo)
Deschampsia	Spartina

IS YOUR SOIL ACID
OR ALKALINE?

It is the underlying rock that determines the nutrient content and the acidity or alkalinity of the soil. At one extreme, the limestone pavements of the Burren in the west of Ireland, stripped bare by glaciation many thousands of years ago, now cradle a remarkable collection of calcium-loving species, such as spring gentians. At the other extreme, in North Wales, the granite flakes and shales of Snowdonia underlie acid soils, where rhododendrons flourish. So much so that one species, *Rhododendron ponticum*, from the Caucasus, has invaded the landscape and reached pest proportions. And the most spectacular part of Hadrian's Wall runs along one of the major geological features of northern England – the Great Whin Sill – a volcanic basalt strip, which again has strong acid soils. The vegetation on the surface clearly shows where the basalt meets the limestone, with rank reeds and matt grasses on one part, and sweet grazing on the other.

Some plants are so typical of lime-rich soil that they are called indicator species – the bird's-foot trefoil (*Lotus corniculatus*) is one. Plants that indicate boggy or marshy ground are those such as the marsh marigold (*Caltha palustris*) and lady's-smock (*Cardamine pratensis*), sometimes called the cuckoo flower. One plant that became common on wartime bomb sites is the rosebay willowherb (*Chamaenerion angustifolium*), which Americans call the fire weed, because it is one of the first plants to colonize burnt ground after a forest fire.

ACID SOILS

If you have very acid soil, there are various strategies open to you. You can select plants that grow on this type of soil, or you can incorporate lime to lower the natural acidity.

Gardeners lime the soil for two principal reasons: first, to try to make the soil more alkaline where it has become extremely acidic, because overly acid soil limits the range of plants you can grow; and, second, because if the soil is heavy clay, with its very fine particles, the lime helps the particles to stick together, creating larger crumbs, which in turn helps to aerate the soil and also improves drainage.

If you think your soil is too acid, do a pH test (see page 29). If it reads four or under on the chart, then your soil will definitely benefit from liming. The best time to lime is in late autumn, and the lime is simply laid over the surface, as the rain will wash it down into the soil. There are various types of lime you can use, but seek advice from your local garden centre on exactly what to buy. Do not apply the lime at the same time as any general fertilizer, and leave the lime on the soil for about eight weeks before adding anything else to it.

Liming can also be helpful in counteracting certain plant problems. For example, if you are growing brassicas and they get club root disease, rather than spending a fortune on various chemical solutions, test the pH of the soil, since acid encourages the formation of the fungal spores that cause the disease. Liming the soil will reduce the chances of it occurring. Quite often the cause of plant disease is the gardener's method of cultivation, and if this is recognized and changed, there will be less need to use potentially harmful chemicals.

BELOW *Some plants have distinct preferences for acid or alkaline soil, such as rhododendrons, which require a neutral to acid soil. Rhododendron ponticum has found the acid soil in parts of Wales and Scotland so much to its liking that it has become an invasive weed.*

PLANTS THAT THRIVE IN ACID SOIL

Our garden plants come from many different parts of the world. Because we are familiar with the plants, we tend to forget that many of them did not originate in the British Isles but were brought back from different corners of the globe, principally in the nineteenth century. In fact, many different regions of the world do have similar growing conditions – even those that we think of as hot and dry have mountainous areas, where the climatic and soil conditions are similar to our own. But when you are planning a collection of plants for your garden, try to consider their original needs, both in terms of soil type and climate.

One of the major problems for the great garden collections that developed at the turn of the century, when plant hunters were bringing back hundreds of new species from different parts of the world, was to find the right conditions for such a wide range of plants. At Mount Usher Gardens near Dublin there is a wonderful range of exotic plants. And what they have in common is a liking for a particular soil type and climate.

Among the hundreds of trees at Mount Usher there is the blue pine (*Pinus montezumae*) from Mexico, a magnificent specimen with great chimneysweep brushes, which grows 21m (70ft) tall. Then from Chile there is the *Eucryphia glutinosa*. Nearby is the cedar from Tasmania, *Athrotaxis cupressoides*, and a

ABOVE *Crinodendrum hookerianum is a wonderfully exotic-looking shrub in full bloom.*

little further away is the Chinese lantern tree (*Crinodendrum hookerianum*).

All these trees thrive on a particular level of acidity (in Mount Usher's case, it is a level of 4.5, and the soil has no peat in it), and have a preference for a temperate climate with plenty of moisture.

TESTING SOIL pH

RIGHT *There are several different types of soil-test kit available which will reveal if your soil is acid or alkaline. They involve using a solution that changes colour when mixed with soil, which can then be matched on a chart to colours, numbered 1 to 14, to read off the pH level of the soil. The optimum for growing most plants is in the range of 5.5 to 7.5. The lower the figure, the more acid the soil. It pays to carry out a pH test when you take on a new garden, because some*

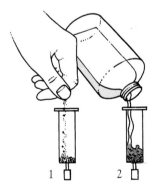
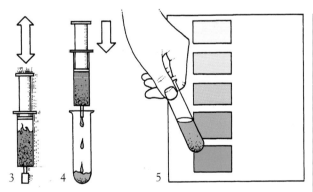

plants, such as rhododendrons, will simply not grow in very alkaline soil.

1 *Put a pH filter in the bottom of the syringe, then*

crumble in a small quantity of soil, which is free of stones.
2 *Add the solution to the soil in the syringe.*
3 *Insert the plunger and shake the syringe.*

4 *Squirt the solution into the test tube, then wait a few seconds.*
5 *Compare the colour of the solution in the tube with the chart to read off the pH level.*

PLANTS THAT REQUIRE ACID SOIL

Calluna	Eucryphia	Gentiana	Lapageria	Pernettya
Camellia	Fothergilla	Heathers	Magnolia	Rhododendron
Erica	Gaultheria	Kalmia	Nyssa	Vaccinium

PLANTS THAT THRIVE IN LIMY SOIL

Acanthus	Cornus	Euonymus	Jasminum	Potentilla
Achillea	Cosmos	Euphorbia	Kniphofia	Pulsatilla
Allium	Cotoneaster	Fagus	Lathyrus	Rosmarinus
Anchusa	Cyclamen	Filipendula	Lupinus	Rudbeckia
Anemone	Cytisus	Forsythia	Lychnis	Salvia
Aquilegia	Dahlia	Fuchsia	Mahonia	Sedum
Arabis	Delphinium	Galanthus	Malus	Sempervivum
Artemisia	Deutzia	Genista	Myosotis	Tradescantia
Bergenia	Dicentra	Geranium	Nemesia	Verbascum
Campanula	Doronicum	Gypsophila	Nepeta	Veronica
Ceanothus	Echinops	Helenium	Nigella	Viburnum
Ceratostigma	Echium	Hemerocallis	Paeonia	Viola
Cheiranthus	Elaeagnus	Hosta	Papaver	Weigela
Clematis	Erigeron	Ilex	Philadelphus	Wisteria
Colchicum	Eryngium	Iris	Phlox	Zinnia

CHALKY SOIL

Most slightly chalky soils are ideal for gardening, with a wide range of plants that can be grown on them. However, very rarely you do get out-crops of pure chalk.

A highly chalky soil is considered by most gardeners to be unplant-able, without considerable effort in terms of adding fertilizers and nutrients. But nature manages to plant up chalkland very successfully. At Byron Down Nature Reserve in Kent the soil is extremely thin over pure chalk, and yet the reserve still manages to play host to up to 30 different species of plant in one square metre of land.

One of the paradoxes of chalk grassland is that the thinner the soil, the richer the plant layer is. Provided that the soil is nutrient-poor and pretty dry as well, you will get an incredibly rich variety of species growing on it, quite in contrast to normal gardening experience. This is because if the soil were rich, one or two species would romp ahead and dominate the others.

If you have a piece of pure chalk outcrop in your garden, you are faced with two alternatives. You can either work extremely hard over the years, and try to fertilize the soil and bring the alkalinity level up to something approaching the norm, or you can make a conscious decision to work with nature, rather than against. You should not expect to grow large blowzy flowers on it, but you can achieve an attractive, colourful carpet of flowers amid thin grass, and even a few shrubs, such as wild privet (*Ligustrum* sp.) and dogroses (*Rosa canina*). Do not make the mistake of fertilizing the soil, however, since all that will do is promote the vigorous, dominating plants that you do not want, such as creeping thistles.

As far as maintaining grass on chalk is concerned, the best bet is to go for a meadow garden approach, leaving the grass to get established for a couple of years and then carrying out a hay cut in September. You should not only cut but take away the cuttings, so that they do not enrich the soil. That way you keep the soil nutrient-poor, and you should cut again in March or April, if the soil has become too rich and growth is getting too vigorous.

Growing in Containers

For various reasons – the soil may be temporarily unworkable, or it may be too acid or too alkaline for the plants you want to grow – you may find it worth while growing plants in containers. This is most likely to be the case if you live in an area of chalky soil and want to grow a lime-hating plant such as the rhododendron.

You can opt either for raised beds (see below) filled with your own growing medium or for containers. Whichever you use, it will have to have a proper drainage system, so that surplus water can flow away easily. Raised beds can be made of many different materials, but bricks, railway-sleepers and concrete blocks are most commonly used. Make sure you create drainage holes in the base of the structure, and add a hardcore or rubble layer before filling the area with the growing medium. You can buy specially formulated composts for acid-loving plants, such as rhododendrons, azaleas, camellias and pieris.

MAKING A RAISED BED
RIGHT *For a raised bed the soil needs to be contained in a sturdy, well-built structure, made from bricks, stone, heavy-duty wooden planks or concrete, built on a hardcore base. A base layer of rubble, with gravel over it, will improve drainage, and a layer of growing medium, thick enough to take the root depth of the chosen plants, should be placed on top. Holes must be left in the base of the raised bed to allow water to drain out.*

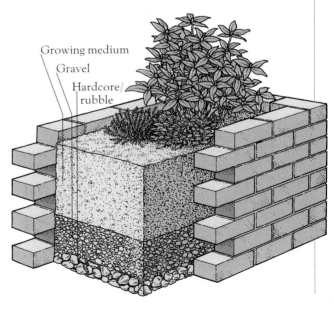

Growing medium

Gravel

Hardcore/ rubble

LOOKING BENEATH THE SURFACE

Few gardeners have much idea about what is actually happening in the soil in their gardens, and quite often in dealing with it they are mistaken about what is – or is not – important. To discover just how different soil structure and composition can be, it is worth taking a closer look at two examples – one a naturally occurring soil, and the other cultivated garden soil. In one, distinct layers are visible in the soil; in the other, they have become mixed. The former deters plant growth, the latter favours it. Your aim, as a gardener, is to create the latter, even if nature has given you the former!

A podzol soil like the one below (the word *podzol* comes from the Russian and roughly translated means 'ash ground') is typical of coniferous vegetation, as it would be of heathland vegetation, and offers a highly acidic environment.

Conifers produce extremely acidic organic matter, which falls on to the soil surface and begins to break down, but the breakdown is slow because of the high level of acidity. Large quantities of un-decomposed organic matter also sit in a thick layer on the surface. From here down, there is a distinct division between the organic material that comes from the conifers above and the mineral matter that has originated from the parent material below, which is a very sandy material, almost white in colour. The two layers are so distinct because of the acidity of the environment. Earthworms cannot live in these conditions, as they find the sand too abrasive, and so the separate layers have not become mixed, because there are no organisms to combine the organic matter with the mineral matter.

On the whole, the soils in Britain are dominated by the downward movement of water. There is enough rain to keep water moving down through this sample all the time, and it is so white because all the

BELOW *In the sample of podzol soil* (LEFT), *which inhibits the growth of most plants, there are very distinct layers. The acidity of the soil has discouraged any earthworm activity and in turn any plant growth; the soil layers remain quite separate, with a hard pan of minerals, washed through the soil layers, forming a crust at the base. In the garden soil sample* (BELOW RIGHT), *to which lots of organic matter has been added, the activity of earthworms has broken down the soil and has created a far deeper layer of topsoil, which is the ideal growing medium for most plants.*

PODZOL SAMPLE

Decomposing acidic matter

Minerals leached into the soil

Iron pan

Underlying rock

GARDEN SOIL SAMPLE

Topsoil with organic matter, well mixed

Subsoil

Underlying rock

ABÒVE *Coniferous forest produces thick layers of highly acidic matter from falling leaves, with the result that little else will grow in the soil beneath the trees' canopies.*

nutrients have been washed out of the top layer. The material is washed down and gets deposited, about 1m (3–4 ft) lower down, and often forms an iron pan, which you can see if you dig down far enough.

By contrast, if you take a garden soil sample, the most distinctive feature is that the organic matter and the mineral matter in the topsoil are thoroughly mixed together, so there is no longer any clear horizon in the soil. This example is far less acidic than the podzol soil sample, and there is considerable earthworm activity, which has been responsible for mixing the two soils together. Again, the subsoil has no organic matter, as earthworm activity generally stops at that point.

If this were a vegetable patch, the topsoil layer would probably be quite a lot deeper, because it would have been cultivated regularly and lots of organic matter added. But if you dig deep enough in any garden soil, you will come down to a subsoil lacking in organic matter.

THE NATURAL CYCLE

In the wild, nature provides a complete cycle of growth and decay that will encourage healthy plant development. The gardener, for his or her sins, usually manages to break this carefully constructed chain by altering the balance of nature. Hence the need in a cultivated garden to add certain chemicals and nutrients to the soil, which would normally have found their way back into it through the remains of dying plants. Nature also occasionally disrupts the pattern herself – heavy rainfall and rapidly draining soil will wash nutrients out of the soil, for example. Since different species adapt to different conditions, you will find that in certain areas particular plants dominate and take over.

The gardener's aim is normally to grow a wide range of different plants successfully, and to do so he occasionally has to give nature a helping hand. For instance, if you grow vegetable crops intensively, the plants will take many of the nutrients out of the soil, because you are pulling them up to eat them, rather than letting the leaves die naturally and be taken back into the soil by earthworms, where they would add to the nitrogen content of the soil. So the vegetable gardener rapidly finds that if he doesn't make up for what he has taken away, his next crop is not as large or as healthy as his first. Eventually, if he did nothing, he would succeed in growing nothing!

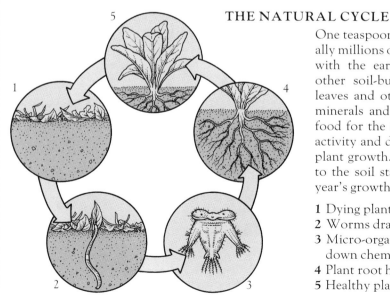

THE NATURAL CYCLE

One teaspoonful of well-fertilized soil contains literally millions of micro-organisms. It is their job, along with the earthworms, millipedes, centipedes and other soil-burrowing insects, to break down the leaves and other dying plant remains so that their minerals and nutrients can be released to provide food for the questing roots of plants. This cycle of activity and dependency is at the root of all healthy plant growth. Failure to return dying plant remains to the soil starves it of essential nutrients for next year's growth.

1 Dying plant remains on the surface of the soil.
2 Worms dragging material into the soil.
3 Micro-organisms (in this case a rotifer) breaking down chemicals.
4 Plant root hairs absorbing nutrients.
5 Healthy plant growth.

NUTRIENTS

The gardener needs, therefore, to think about adding nutrients to the soil wherever the soil is naturally poor, the ground is being intensively cultivated, or particular parts of the plant are being grown for consumption or for specific qualities – large crops of flowers, and so on.

Botanists have categorized the nutrients into major and minor ones. The major nutrients for plant growth are nitrogen, phosphate and potash (which bear the symbols N, P and K respectively). They each affect different aspects of the plant's growth. If you are growing leaf vegetables such as lettuces and spring cabbages, for example, you want rapid growth, and you should therefore supply the plant with extra nitrogen to enable it to achieve this. If the plant is to produce flowers and fruit, then you need to add extra amounts of phosphate and potash.

In normal gardening circumstances – for instance, in the herbaceous border – if you allow plants to die down naturally and do not cart the remains away, these essential nutrients are fed back into the soil and you will need to add little in the way of top dressing. Beneath the soil,

TABLE OF MAIN FERTILIZERS: CHEMICAL COMPOSITION AND USE

| NAME | CONTENT % | | | RATE | USE | WHEN TO |
	N_2	P_2O	K_2O	per sq. m.		APPLY
Basic slag	—	17	—	225 g (8 oz)	All green vegetables	Autumn/winter
Bone meal	4	20	—	200 g (7 oz)	All green vegetables	Autumn/winter
Dried blood	7–14	2·0	1	25 g (1 oz)	Pot plants, lettuce	Spring/summer
Growmore	7·0	7·0	7·0	50 g (2 oz)	A safe general fertilizer	Spring/summer
Nitrate of soda	16	—	—	25 g (1 oz)	All green vegetables	Spring/summer
Poultry manure	4·0	5·0	3	110 g (4 oz)	Best mixed in compost	Growing season
Sewage sludge (dried)	2·0	1·5	0·1	225 g (8 oz)	A good soil conditioner	Autumn/winter
Sulphate of ammonia	20	—	—	15 g (½ oz)	All green vegetables	Spring/summer
Sulphate of potash	—	—	50	25 g (1 oz)	All green vegetables	All year
Superphosphates	—	20	—	50 g (2 oz)	All green vegetables	Spring/summer
Wood ash		4·0	25		Use occasionally on fruit and flowers	Autumn
Farmyard manure	0·2	0·4	0·5	4·5 kg (10 lb)	A general soil improver	Autumn
Garden compost	2·0	1·0	0·5	4·5 kg (10 lb)	Apply to all, especially sandy, soils	Summer/autumn
Leaf mould	2	0·1	—	2·25 kg (5 lb)	An excellent soil conditioner	Autumn/summer
Peat	1·5	0·1	0·1	2·25–4·5 kg (5–10 lb)	Little food value, but good for light soils	Summer
Seaweed	0·2	—	1·5		A soil conditioner and source of trace elements	Winter/spring
Spent hops	3·5	1·0	trace	1 kg (2 lb)	Should be mixed with 1 kg (2 lb) Growmore per 50 kg (1 cwt) of hops	Summer

nature is labouring for you, doing the work of fertilizing your plants, helped by the rainfall as it washes surface materials down through the soil. The dying plant remains are being broken up and eaten by worms, woodlice, beetles and bacteria. Many of the so-called garden pests are actually working on your behalf, although occasionally they get into the wrong place at the wrong time – earwigs into the buds of flowers, for example.

If a leaf falls off a plant and dies, various insects will start chewing the softer parts and you will eventually be left with the veins. Bacteria will in turn cause this to rot, and these rotting remains help to form the humus that all gardeners so revere for the rich, nutritious element that it adds to the soil.

THE NITROGEN CYCLE

When organic matter is incorporated into the soil and broken down, complex changes take place. At first nitrogen – although present in the soil – is not available to the plant, and it is said to be immobilized. Over a period of time, further chemical changes occur and the nitrogen is converted into a form that plants are able to extract from the soil and use to promote and sustain growth.

Nitrogen for garden soils is provided by such materials as fertilizers, plant residues, manures, and ammonium and nitrates carried down in rain and irrigation water. Some plants, such as legumes (members of the pea family), and certain micro-organisms also have the capacity to extract nitrogen from the Earth's atmosphere.

The loss of nitrogen from garden soils can occur in several ways: it may be used by plants to sustain growth; leached out of the soil as the water drains away; carried away when soil erosion occurs; and nitrogen gas can be released back into the atmosphere.

NUTRIENT DEFICIENCY

For a variety of reasons, the nutritional balance in the soil can go awry, but this is generally due to the gardener's interference with nature's scheme. If you religiously made compost and applied it to your garden regularly and systematically, this problem should not arise. People often rush to the chemical cupboard at the first signs of damage or disease on plants (see table on page 35), but chemical fertilizers are not always all that they are cracked up to be. Chemically fertilized crops are often lush, but they are also weak and prone to disease. And the gardener then gets trapped in a vicious cycle of applying pesticides, fungicides and bacteriocides.

It is far better to work *with* the soil, and your plants, in the first place, putting back into the soil what you have taken out in the form of compost, rather than reaching for the medicine cabinet.

ABOVE *Plants are capable of absorbing carbon dioxide from the air, which is processed into carbohydrates by photosynthesis, in which oxygen is given off by the plant. The plant also needs nitrogen in large amounts and absorbs it from the soil through its roots. When the plant dies and the remains return to the soil, these remains provide the nitrogen for the next cycle of growth.*

SYMPTOMS OF SOIL DEFICIENCY

SYMPTOM	ELEMENT DEFICIENCY
Leaves appear chlorotic (pale green or yellow colour); older leaves turn yellow at the tips; leaf margins remain green but yellowing occurs down the mid-ribs.	Nitrogen
Plants are stunted and dark green in colour; older leaves develop a purple hue.	Phosphorus
Unnatural shortening of plant internodes (areas of stem between the nodes, or swellings in grasses and sweet corn); leaf tips turn yellow and appear scorched.	Potassium
Older leaves turn yellow and then develop whitish stripes between the leaf veins.	Magnesium
New leaves develop whitish areas at the base on each side of the mid-rib; internodes appear shortened.	Zinc
Plants develop general chlorosis of the leaves.	Sulphur
Mottled effect on new leaves; in apples, a spotty chlorosis appears between the lateral leaf veins, and the chlorotic areas die, leaving holes.	Manganese
Brassica plants particularly show cupping, an inward curling of the leaves, and the leaf tips become wrinkled.	Molybdenum
Root crops, especially turnips and swedes, turn grey and mushy at their centres.	Boron

MULCHING

Mulch is used for two reasons: first, for weed control, where it is extremely effective against annual weeds and, if you use black plastic as well, against perennial ones, too (see page 154); second, as a means of conserving moisture. For the mulch to do its job effectively it must be at least 10cm (4in) thick. If it is much thinner than that, it tends to blow about. In any case, if you are using an organic mulch, the layer closest to the soil will be gradually broken down by bacterial activity.

Mulches are quite expensive, so you need to find a compromise. One solution is to look around your area for waste products that are cheap. More or less anything can be used as a mulch – seaweed, spent mushroom compost, old carpet – but ideally it should not look unsightly. We are now seeing the organic residues of plants from other parts of the world shipped in to make mulch – coconut shells, for example, are being ground up to make an alternative to peat, which is running dangerously short. And in parts of the United States, peanut shells are being used as a mulch, apparently successfully.

If you have a largish garden, and do a lot of pruning, then it makes sense to hire a chipper to strip all the clippings into small bits for mulch, rather than chuck it away on a skip or burn it.

Lighter materials will need to be composted, otherwise they blow around too much and you lose the layers too quickly. If you compost the material (see page 39) and leave it for a year before using it, it makes an excellent mulch. You can then get away with laying it much thinner than usual (about 5cm/2in thick) if you spread it over plastic sheeting.

MULCHES

	AVAILABILITY	APPLICATION	DURABILITY	ADVANTAGES	DISADVANTAGES
Bark	Becoming available in many garden stores or direct from mills	Shrubberies and borders	Top up every 2 years.	Looks attractive and improves the structure of the soil.	Must be well fermented. Does not add nutrients.
Compost	Can be made in any garden	Anywhere	Renew annually.	Improves both the fertility of the soil and its structure.	Takes time and effort to make.
Creeping plants	Universal	Beneath trees and shrubs	Long-term, but can be wiped out rapidly by pests or disease.	The most attractive weed suppressant.	Take a long time to become really effective.
Manure	Freely available in rural areas	Anywhere	Dissipates quickly.	Improves and enriches the soil.	If not well rotted, it can be acid and smelly; it introduces weed seeds into the garden.
Peat	Available	In shrubberies and in borders	Loses roughly 15 per cent of its volume every year.	Improves soil structure. Looks good.	Blows about when dry.
Plastic	Universal	Shrubberies	Long-term.	Excellent weed suppressant.	Unsightly and needs covering. Does not add nutrients.
Sawdust	Easy to obtain	Borders and shrubberies	Top up annually.	Very easy to spread.	Can be used only if it has been fermented for 12 months. Blows away easily. Does not add nutrients.
Seaweed	Available only near the sea	Anywhere	Lasts only a season.	Good source of humus and trace elements.	Must be well composted before use.
Spent hops	Available from breweries	Anywhere	Renew annually.	Has an attractive texture and quickly improves soil structure.	Tend to blow about on windy sites.
Spent mushroom compost	Easily obtainable from mushroom farms	Anywhere	Renew annually.	Fine source of humus.	Very short duration; only suitable for lime-tolerant plants.
Spent tomato compost	Easily obtainable from professional growers	Anywhere	Renew annually.	Improves soil texture.	Blows about when dries out. High levels of fertilizer residue.
Straw	Easily available	Most suited to vegetable gardens	Renew annually.	Cheap enough to use copiously.	Looks messy, may carry weed seed and can only be used if supplementary nitrogenous fertilizer is added.

Provided that you make a slight depression in the soil at the point where the plants are inserted, the rainwater will run down into the planting holes, so that the plastic does not act – as you might suppose – to prevent the water from reaching the plants. In fact, any kind of plastic sheeting will do, and if it is covered with mulch and not exposed to sunlight, it will last for up to 15 years, since it is sunlight that eventually degrades plastic.

One thing that you must be careful about with most forms of mulch is not to allow the mulching material to butt right up to the stem of the plant. Active forms of mulch – such as wood chippings or grass cuttings – generate considerable heat, and if they get too close to the plant they will actually scorch it. Ideally, leave a 5cm (2in) gap between the plant and the mulch.

GARDEN COMPOST

Recycling garden waste and household vegetable matter is not only ecologically sound but, if incorporated, it makes a huge difference to the structure of most soils, turning unworkable clay or droughty sand into good loam. It also provides the plants with all the nutrients they require. How much compost you make depends to some extent on the size of your garden, the quantity of household waste you can contribute and how much time you are prepared to spend. With the exception of horse manure – itself a form of composted grass – there is no really good alternative, however, and anyone who wants to grow plants successfully should be prepared to make compost. Since compost is composed of rotting vegetable matter, you may wonder why you need

MAKING A COMPOST BIN

You can make your own compost bin with whatever bits of timber you have lying around. If you do not have enough timber for the sides, you can use chicken wire instead.

Get two timber battens of equal length and a piece of board at least 1m (3ft) long – old skirting board is ideal for this. Nail the board across the battens. Then add planks to create the height you want. Leave a bit of space between each plank in order to allow the air to circulate.

Create another side and the back of your compost bin, then nail an extra batten on each side at the front, so that you can insert the planks between the battens. This permits the front planks to be removed, if necessary, by pushing them up, in order to fork compost out from the base of the heap.

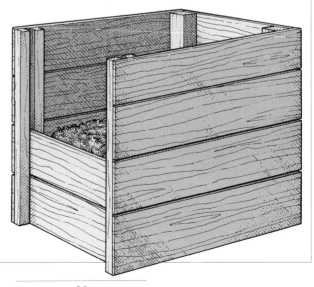

Mulches are of great use to the gardener, none more so than bark chippings (LEFT) in a border, or black plastic (BELOW) for growing broad beans. Both of these suppress or, in the case of plastic, inhibit the growth of weeds. The only disadvantages of plastic are that it is unsightly and impermeable. In the vegetable garden this is less important. In a border, a combination of plastic covered with a thin layer of bark chippings makes a practical, and attractive, weed suppressor.

to go to the bother of making a great heap of it, rather than simply spreading it around the garden. The answer is that the bacteria that break down the plant material use up a lot of nitrogen in the process. If you dig vegetable matter straight into the soil, the bacteria lock up the nitrates that the plants also need, and this can create a temporary nitrogen deficiency. If you create a compost heap, you do not starve the soil of nitrogen in the rotting process. The bacterial activity also generates heat, which may scorch plant roots and cause severe damage or even death to some plants.

There are as many methods of making compost as there are gardeners, but the aim of all of them is, first, to get the vegetable matter to rot efficiently and, second, to produce enough for the garden's needs.

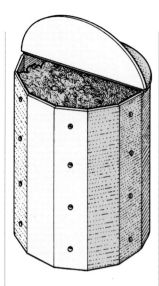

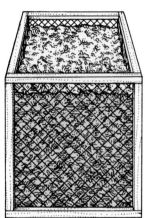

ABOVE *Compost bins can be bought ready-made, like the plastic cylindrical bin, which is useful for small gardens, or you can make a simple version out of chicken wire nailed to a basic wooden frame.*

So how does compost work? The idea is to make a large enough heap of decaying vegetable matter that it actually heats up, thereby killing any pests and diseases and speeding up the rotting process. Although you can make a compost heap completely naturally, you can also add a proprietary compost activator or manure to speed up the process.

There are a few points worth bearing in mind. If the compost heap is too dry, the bacteria involved in the rotting process will not be able to work; and if the heap gets too wet, or too hot, then the bacteria get killed off. So compost-making has its finer points. For the ideal compost heap you need a good balance of different ingredients – grass clippings after you have mown the lawn, vegetable waste from the house, prunings from plants, dead leaves in autumn. Turned over regularly, these will combine, making a rich and fertile mixture to spread on the soil. Air is another element in the composting process. Without it, the heap heats up too much and kills the bacteria that are supposed to be doing the work for you. Avoid, therefore, overly thick layers of grass clippings or of other materials.

You can hire chippers to shred wood and prunings for the compost heap, but take care not to overdo it, and mix these in with other vegetable waste. Conifer bark, for example, contains terpenoid compounds that are used in making turpentine substitutes, and it tends to produce high levels of these in the bark-composting process. These are very toxic to plants, as was found to one gardener's cost when bark was used as an alternative to peat – the effect was rather like dipping the roots of the plants in neat turpentine.

The secret, then, of good composting is rather like that of good health in humans: a balanced diet. As a general warning, compost that is too rich in nitrogen smells of ammonia and compost that lacks air smells of rotten eggs.

When the compost is ready – it normally takes about three months – it has a crumbly, dark brown consistency and smells sweet! It is often good practice to have two compost bins on the go; one with compost that you are in the process of making, and another that you are taking from. If you make slats that lift up at the front of the compost container, you can make do with one bin, which is added to at the top and taken from at the base.

COMPOST HEAPS AND BINS

Although there is nothing to prevent you from simply making a compost pile in the corner of your garden, a purpose-made bin will speed up the process by ensuring that the compost is well aerated. It will also look much tidier, as well as being easier to deal with. You can either make your own compost bin (again, there are dozens of models, one of which is illustrated above) or you can buy a proprietary one.

DIGGING THE GARDEN

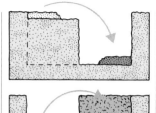
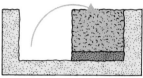

You dig the soil for two reasons: first, to improve aeration; second, to incorporate organic matter and fertilizers in order to add nutrients to the soil. Land that has been badly neglected will need to be cleared before it can be dug. Normally, on a very overgrown plot, a strimmer will be needed to slash down the vegetation or, if you have the energy, you can use a scythe. Burn all the perennial weeds and then set about digging over the plot.

Generally, systematic single digging is necessary for this kind of job (see right). It gives you the opportunity to add compost or fertilizer to the soil, and ensures that the soil has been dug to a uniform level over the entire plot.

On less overgrown ground, you can usually get away with simple digging. In other words, turning the soil over with a spade or fork. Using a fork has the advantage that it does not chop up the roots of perennial weeds, which will re-sprout if you do not remove all the tiny

SINGLE DIGGING
ABOVE *Dig a trench about one spade's depth down and about 30cm (12in) wide. Working backwards, dig another trench immediately behind the first and pile the soil into the newly dug trench. Remove any perennial weeds, but turn over annual weeds into the base of the trench in front.*

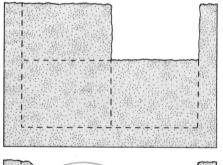

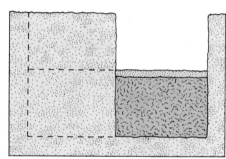

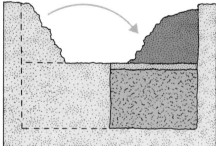

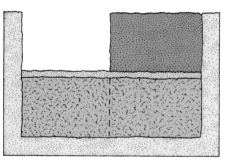

DOUBLE DIGGING
Dig according to the plan (LEFT), taking out two spades' depth of soil from each trench, and shovelling it into the newly dug trench in front as you work. If the topsoil is shallow, do not mix the different depths of soil, but shovel the top layer of soil on to the base layer of the trench in front.

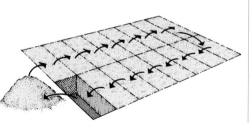

RIGHT *To dig the ground efficiently, mark out the bed as shown, and dig a series of trenches, working backwards and filling the newly dug trench in front with the soil of the trench being worked on, as shown by the arrows.*

DARWIN AND THE EARTHWORM

After his epic voyage on the *Beagle*, and after publishing *On the Origin of Species* in 1859, Charles Darwin continued researching a subject that would involve him in some 40 years of observation, experiment and thought: the part played in the history of the world by the humble earthworm. In the garden of his home at Down House in Kent, Darwin set up an experiment to measure how worms can undermine stones and cause them to sink. In fact, although the experiment never really worked, the observations expounded in his last book, *Vegetable Mould and Earthworms*, were profound. Darwin concluded that the plough is one of the most ancient and valuable of man's inventions, but, long before man existed, the land was in fact regularly ploughed – and continued to be thus ploughed – by earthworms. It is marvellous to reflect that the whole of the Earth's superficial mould has passed, and will pass again, through the bodies of worms every few years. Darwin also calculated that, in many parts of Britain, on 0.4ha (1 acre) of ground a weight of more than 10 ton(ne)s of earth passes annually through the bodies of worms. That is not so surprising, when it has been calculated that the weight of worms below the ground is equivalent to that of a dairy herd above. In the garden, no matter how carefully the soil is dug and hoed, the same underground helpers are still blindly at work, turning the soil for their own – and our – benefit.

pieces. However, you cannot physically move the soil from one place to another with a fork, and on heavy clay soil you may find that a spade is the only suitable tool.

A more drastic form of single digging – double digging – is sometimes required on previously uncultivated land – for example, where the garden of a house was formerly a field. This entails digging down two spades' depth in a series of trenches. But in areas where the topsoil is shallow, you have to ensure that you do not bring the subsoil to the surface (see left).

NO-DIG SYSTEM

These days some people prefer to operate a 'no-dig' system of cultivation. The aim is to incorporate all the organic material needed for the soil in one double-digging operation, and then to leave the soil more or less undisturbed. The argument in favour of this system runs that cultivation of the soil paradoxically creates conditions in which weeds flourish, and also damages the natural structure of the soil. In order to operate this system successfully, the soil must not be compacted again (in other words, do not walk on it) and it must be in first-class condition after having been double-dug.

MAKING A SEEDBED

Seeds need plenty of air in the soil if they are to germinate successfully (see page 99). Soil in which seeds are to be sown therefore has to be much finer in texture than normal garden soil, and all stones, bits of twig and clods of soil should be broken down. Then rake over the soil, leave the seedbed for a month before sowing, and rake again. Water well before and after sowing, using the fine rose on a watering can.

THE HIDDEN PLANT

The underground parts of the plant do not excite the interest of most gardeners, unless they are growing root crops for food. There are, however, a couple of important points to make about them. First, not all underground parts of the plant are actually roots – bulbs, tubers, corms and rhizomes are, in fact, other parts of the plant (stems or leaf bases) that simply happen to be underground. To some extent, this is a matter of semantics, since roots are in reality underground shoots, and root and shoot growth are balanced to take advantage of the different aspects of the natural environment.

Roots, normally underground and therefore rarely seen, have adapted in various ways over the centuries. On the Sang Dragon tree (Pterocarpus indica) (BELOW) buttress roots have formed above ground level to give additional support to the trunk of the tree.
On epiphytes, such as Tillandsia ionantha 'Scaposa' (LEFT), aerial roots have evolved, which enable the plant to live in a soil-less environment, often on the branches of trees in their native tropical rain forests.

It is important to remember that roots are every bit as essential as shoots. Being hidden from view, they are often forgotten about, or at best ignored, and yet the root is the plant's primary source of nourishment. If the roots fail, the plant will fail, as the gardener often finds to his cost, when a container-grown plant that has stood neglected in the garden becomes root-bound (see page 55).

Roots actually perform three functions for the plant: first, they anchor the plant in the soil; second, they absorb water and nutrients from it; and, third, they store food for the plant for later use.

Roots exist below the soil surface because that is the environment in which they normally function best. Nature being what it is, there are exceptions, and plants have adapted over the millennia to different conditions. Epiphytes (the word comes from the Greek *epi*, meaning 'upon', and *phytum*, meaning 'plant') cling to tree branches in the tropical rain forest and live in a soil-less environment, their roots adapted principally for support. As a result, they have had to undergo changes to enable them to collect the moisture they require. Instead of the root hairs of most underground plants (see page 48), which serve this purpose, some species of epiphytic orchids, for example, have aerial roots covered in a soft white tissue called velamen, which is capable of absorbing not only water but even water vapour.

Other plants have also acquired aerial rather than underground roots. Climbers such as ivy (*Hedera* sp.) have small aerial roots emerging from their stems, and they use these to cling to almost any surface with which they are in contact, penetrating into tiny cracks and crevices in bark and brickwork. They also exude a powerful adhesive, so that they can attach themselves to perfectly smooth surfaces like glass. Contrary to popular belief, ivy is no longer the threat it once was to brickwork. People used to say that if ivy grew up a house, the roots would eat into the mortar in their search for moisture. It is true that they will do so, if the mortar in question is based on lime putty (as it was in old houses), but they cannot penetrate the cement-based mortar used on modern houses.

Yet another strange adaptation is that of buttress roots. Since the tallest plants do not necessarily have the deepest roots, some plants have developed an anchoring root system. Known as buttress roots, these exist principally to support the plant rather than to search for nourishment. They are often seen on trees in the tropical rain forest, where the search for light, and the lack of water, has created incredibly tall trees with a shallow root system, which need extra support. These massive buttress roots sometimes extend 6m (20ft) or more up the trunk of the tree. Those of the Honduras mahogany tree (*Swietenia mahagoni*) are enormous, reaching just such a height. On a much smaller scale, sweet corn (*Zea mays*) has developed a system of buttress roots, although these lie below ground. Maize is pollinated by the wind and its fruit is fairly heavy, so to prevent the plant from toppling over in its efforts to get pollinated – and to help it to bear the load of the fruit, once set – the plant has developed a system of buttress roots. In prevailing windy conditions, the buttress roots form on the leeward side to counteract the effects of the wind.

Any living structure, including plant roots, must have air in order to breathe and function, and usually there is sufficient air in the small spaces between the soil particles. However, there are instances where plants have evolved to survive successfully in permanently airless soil conditions, such as mangrove swamps. The mangrove tree (*Rhizophora* sp.) has some roots that grow upwards into the air, enabling the whole root system to breathe.

FIBROUS AND TAP ROOT SYSTEMS

Roots anchor the plant in the soil either by occupying a large volume of soil just below the surface, or by probing deep down beneath it. The roots that occupy the area near the soil surface are called fibrous roots and are profuse and thin. Plants with fibrous roots, particularly grasses, are extremely useful for combating soil erosion, since they create a dense mat that binds the particles of soil together. Fibrous roots enmesh the soil as it moves downwards, and they will rapidly increase in dry periods, so that there is as great a chance as possible of collecting moisture. A tap root system, on the other hand, works in reverse; it sends the root downwards, deep into the soil, to 'tap' the deep water tables and mineral supplies. Plants with tap roots are particularly well anchored against shifting soils and gales. Some plant species have one root system, some the other; and some can adopt one form or the other, depending on the prevailing conditions, producing fibrous roots when the soil is moist and tap roots when it is dry.

Although food is stored in both types of roots, tap roots have a far greater storage capacity, since they enlarge in girth as well as in length. Man has taken advantage of this ability of tap roots to store foods. In the case of carrots, for example, he harvests the plant at the time when the tap root has its greatest storage capacity. Left to its own devices, the carrot's reserves of nutrients in the tap root would serve to provide it with the energy to create flowers and seed the following year. When the tops of biennial and perennial plants die back in autumn, their reserves of food come from their roots, which provide them with the means to create new foliage the following spring.

Most garden plants have relatively shallow roots, up to a maximum of about 2m (6ft) in length; but many wild plants have massive tap roots, sometimes up to 10m (30ft) deep, and some desert shrubs can grow tap roots up to 30m (90ft) long. Cacti, however, have fibrous roots that take advantage of the rain near the surface before it percolates downwards and is lost.

When tap roots become damaged, the plant responds by developing a multi-branched root system, with four or five roots of more or less equal size replacing the one very thick dominant tap root (the same effect as that created by pruning a stem and removing the apical bud).

Many trees, such as beech (*Fagus sylvatica*) and ash (*Fraxinus excelsior*), develop a long tap root with few lateral roots, when grown from seed. This will be the dominant root system for about the first 25 years of the tree's life. After this period the balance gradually changes, as the tap root often dies back and the lateral roots develop a massive root plate of large, relatively shallow roots (this can often be seen when a mature tree is blown over in a gale).

ABOVE *Although roots look fairly smooth to the naked eye, when photographed in close-up they can be seen to be covered with fine root hairs, which enable them to carry out their task of absorbing minerals and nutrients from the soil.*

How Roots Grow

The underground plant has a vital and dynamic role to play in the everyday functioning of the plant, absorbing minerals and water and passing them on to the network of vessels and veins that link the root tip with the flower bud. Roots and stems are often thought of as separate entities growing in opposite directions, and yet root and shoot growth are balanced. As local environmental changes affect one part of the plant, the other responds in sympathy. The cycles of life depend on this precisely controlled interaction between leaves, stems and roots.

Most people are not even aware that roots grow at all, until their hidden strength suddenly heaves apart a pavement, cracks a drain or brings down a wall.

All of the root's primary growth activities are concentrated in a region about 7mm (¼ in) from its tip, called the apical meristem (see also page 127). The length of the root is increased by the division of cells in the meristem, and when the cells subsequently elongate, the root tip pushes its way forward through the soil with considerable force. Since a damaged meristem cannot be regenerated (although other branches of the root will take on its work), the root tip produces cells ahead of itself to form a protective root cap. When the root-cap cells are ruptured by soil particles, the contents form a slimy coat, which lubricates the root's tip as it passes through the soil.

A short way back from the meristem is an area that looks slightly fuzzy to the naked eye. This fuzziness is caused by hundreds of root hairs, whose job it is to increase the absorptive surface of the root. During periods of root growth, new root hairs are constantly being formed, as old ones die. Roots also grow branches, in the same way that new shoots are produced on the upper parts of the plant. Each has the same cell structure, with its own apical meristem, root hairs and capacity to form root branches.

THE QUESTING ROOT

From the gardener's point of view – as opposed to the plant's – roots are both beneficial and a nuisance. Beneficial in the sense that they help to improve soil structure by holding it together, particularly in light sandy soil; a nuisance in the sense that it is very difficult to find much that will grow under a canopy of large trees, partly because of the shade cast by the leaves, but mostly because the roots absorb a great deal of the moisture and nutrients from the soil.

LAWN GRASSES

What we often fail to realize is how much we, as gardeners, can influence the activity of the roots of plants in our gardens. Take a lawn, for example. If you watered it on an almost daily basis in summer, you would encourage a large amount of surface rooting to take place,

RIGHT *Regular cutting of grass, a plant with a very fibrous root system, encourages new buds to form, so that the lawn becomes thick and dense – the emerald-green sward so revered in our parks and gardens.*

because the roots would form in the areas of soil where the moisture collects. If, instead, you used a pipe inserted through the soil at a depth of about 15cm (6in), you would find that the roots would be drawn down to the source of the water.

Lawns have an immensely fibrous root system. There are probably 10 or 15 times as many roots as there are blades of grass on top. In fact, if you tried to tear up a piece of turf, it would sound like ripping paper, so dense is the mat of fibrous roots below the surface.

Another aspect of lawn grass that we do not consider very often is that the grasses we use have a method of vegetative production, which creates the dense, close mass of green leaves that we like to see. As tufted perennials, these grasses spread by means of underground stems producing a mass of leafy shoots. This all occurs below the surface of

RIGHT *Mowing a lawn actually encourages the grass to grow, because the leaves re-sprout from the base. Removing the tips of the leaves (a) has much the same effect as pruning a shrub, as the growth hormones are diverted to the shoots (b) lower down the plant.*

WORKING IN PARTNERSHIP

An interesting example of benevolent co-existence in which roots are involved is seen in the symbiotic relationship between certain soil fungi and the tender young roots of peas, apples, poplar, oak, birch, pine and some conifers.

Conifers, for example, grow on very acid soil, which tends to lock up the phosphates that the conifer needs for the production of healthy shoots. Certain fungi that live on the roots of these trees are capable of extracting phosphates from the soil and passing these on to the conifer. In turn, the conifer provides carbohydrates (through photosynthesis, see page 66) that the fungi cannot obtain, and so by working in close relationship both plants not only survive, but thrive.

All living things require nitrogen. It makes up 80 per cent of the atmosphere, and yet few organisms can convert the gas into a form that is usable. In another mutually beneficial relationship, a bacterium called rhizobium invades the young roots of receptive plants, such as beans. These bacteria are capable of converting nitrogen into a usable form for the bean, passing it to the root's cells. In return, the host plant, as before, supplies the bacteria with carbohydrates.

As a consequence, plants that encourage this relationship become extremely rich in nitrogen, making them a useful crop to grow on nitrogen-poor soils.

RIGHT *The nodules on these broad bean roots are actually a rich store-house of nitrogen, created by the bacterium rhizobium, which invades the roots in its search for carbohydrates.*

Clover, soya bean and alfalfa are among the plants whose roots are invaded by the rhizobium bacteria and are therefore very useful crops for this purpose.

The other side of the coin is that some plants (known as allelopaths) emit certain chemicals, either through their roots or via fallen leaves and twigs, which make it impossible for other plants to grow nearby, effectively preventing competing plants from taking up nearby resources. The rhododendron is one such plant, and so is the walnut, and it is rare to find other plants growing underneath them. It is hoped that allelopathy may prove useful in the development of organic, environmentally friendly weedkillers derived from natural plant extracts.

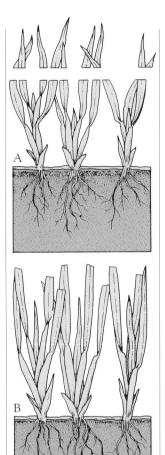

ABOVE *Grasses such as marram grass* (Ammophila arenaria) *have a dense mass of fibrous roots. These can be extremely beneficial in windswept areas with sandy soil, as they help to bind the soil particles together.*

RHIZOMES FOR GROUND COVER

Aegopodium
Arundinaria
Bergenia
Convallaria majalis
Geranium
Hakonechloa
Iris foetidissima
Luzula
Matteuccia
Peltiphyllum peltatum
Phalaris arundinacea
Polygonatum multiflorum
Rodgersia
Schizostylis

the lawn, and the cutting of the leaves above ground simply prevents the production of flowering stems and encourages more buds into shoots, thereby thickening and improving the quality of the lawn.

It is therefore more beneficial to cut the lawn frequently (twice weekly, for example), helping to increase these buds, than to mow only once a fortnight. Fortunately, although lawn grasses sprout from the base, most broad-leaved plants do not, so that regular mowing encourages the grass, but keeps down the weeds.

GROUND-COVER PLANTS

Spreading masses of fibrous roots can also be used to keep down weeds in the garden in other ways, by covering the ground with your own choice of plants rather than nature's. Any plants that spread by means of rhizomes are useful in this respect. Rhizomes are modified stems growing just below the soil surface, and at each leaf joint (node) shoots develop and emerge above the soil, forming a dense mat of foliage very rapidly. Given the right conditions, these plants can quickly spread to make a valuable weed-proof carpet.

TREE ROOTS

Contrary to popular belief, the root system of a tree is surprisingly shallow. A tree 30m (100ft) tall will probably have a root system that goes no deeper than 3m (10ft). What may also surprise some people is that roots need oxygen, and without it they will simply die. Since the nutrients that the roots also need are not found at great depths in the soil, the tree's roots spread outwards in search of these, rather than downwards. There is no hard-and-fast limit to their spread, although you can assume that the roots of a broad-crowned tree will spread as far as its branches. With columnar, forest-grown trees, the roots will often spread to a distance equal to the height of the tree.

Roots, as we have seen, have three purposes: support, nutrition and storage. The support zone of the tree's roots is surprisingly small – for example, a pillar of earth only 3m (10ft) across can support a broad-crowned tree up to 20m (65ft) tall. At Kew Gardens a 70-year-old conifer appears to thrive in a lime-based mortar in a wall and, although stunted to a fraction of its potential growth, endures untended in a seemingly barren environment.

The search for food is carried out by a criss-crossing network of fine roots, bearing root hairs, whose job it is to absorb the moisture and minerals that the tree needs. These fine branch roots run near the soil surface to take advantage of the air, water and nutrients at that level. Unlike supporting roots, they are not permanent, and after a year or two they wither and decay, while new roots grow.

HOW ROOTS GROW

It is at harvest-time on the allotment that gardeners become most aware of the extent of annual root growth. Yet there is a place where it is possible to observe roots flourishing in their subterranean world at any time of the year. A study of the world of roots is being undertaken by Horticultural Research International at its fruit station in East Malling, in Kent. An underground bunker, with a series of observation panels with thick glass between the panels and the soil, allows scientists to observe roots in action without digging up the trees. The first observation panels were built in 1961, and a modified version was constructed in 1966.

Using these panels, scientists can observe how roots travel, how much growth they make at specific times of the year, and so on. Roots tend to take the line of least resistance – former root runs, worm casts, etc. Their object is to push outwards and downwards in search of minerals, nutrients and moisture. There is quite a turnover of roots and a cyclical pattern to their activity, with a flush of growth early in spring and another late in autumn.

The power of roots can be seen where, in one panel, the pressure that a major root has exerted has broken the plate glass. When a root rams its way through the soil, the pressure is considerable, but it cannot go into holes in the soil that are smaller than it is. Although it may have started off as a very small root in a small hole, as the root grows and expands, it fills the hole and starts to push away the surround.

RIGHT *Tree roots can adapt to apparently inhospitable habitats, squeezing themselves into crevices in stones, as here, and exerting enough pressure to force up paving stones and demolish walls.*

Root growth is seasonal, but less so than that of shoots, with most of the growth in spring and summer, normally slowing down in winter. All root growth stops in freezing conditions.

Roots appear to employ an uncanny sense of direction as they tunnel through the soil in search of water and nutrients. They are inexplicably drawn towards the layer of condensation that forms beneath kerbstones and on the outer surfaces of cool pipes. Thereafter they will infiltrate and exploit any crack or weakness in the system.

PLANTING

It is important to remember, when planting, that you must create the best possible conditions for the plant's future growth. Once you know that growth takes place at certain times of the year and the plant needs to remain in balance – in other words, its roots are as important as its branches – and that any interruption to the natural growth process comes as a severe shock to the plant, you begin to understand why

PLANTING A TREE

1 *Dig a generous-sized hole and insert a stake for the tree.*
2 *Plant the tree, spreading out the roots.*
3 *Backfill the hole with soil, firm it in, tie the tree to a stake and water it well.*

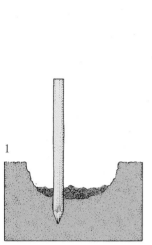

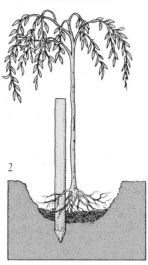

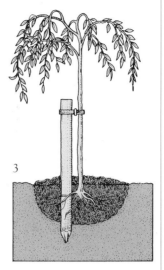

your newly planted rose, for example, simply sits there and looks at you, if you fail to treat it properly.

The first rule is to dig a large enough hole for the plant. Most gardeners are by nature lazy, or else too busy, and so when the plant starts to haunt them, they whizz into the garden, dig a very small hole, stuff the plant in, possibly water it if they are feeling particularly virtuous, and wait for developments. Probably not a lot will happen. With a stout constitution, and moderately good soil, the plant will survive, but it will certainly fail to grow at its normal rate.

So what should you do, and why? The first principle is to plant at a time when the plant is not heavily engaged in other activities, so autumn and winter are the best times for planting. Second, the hole you make should be large enough, and loose enough round the edges for the soil to be inviting to the roots; it should encourage them to explore for food, not prevent them from doing so. Third, help the roots by spreading them out in the right direction, rather than leaving them in the strait-jacket provided by the container. Finally, firm the plant in, to make sure that it is solidly based, not rocking in the wind. And give it plenty to drink, to make up for the shock of being moved.

ROOT PRUNING

Since root and shoot growth are connected, it is obvious that if you restrict the growth of the roots, you restrict that of the shoots. Root pruning is sometimes used to control over-vigorous shrubs.

MOVING A TREE OR LARGE SHRUB

ABOVE *Start a year ahead of the move, when the plant is dormant. The bigger the tree or shrub, the larger the root ball you need to leave in place.*

About 1m (3ft) from the tree, start digging a trench about 30cm (12in) wide and 60cm (24in) deep. Cut through any roots as neatly as you can, and then slowly cut under the tree as well. Ideally, try to wrap up the roots in black plastic sheeting. Move the plant to its new site, and plant as above. You should incorporate a stake before you plant the tree, so that you do not damage the tree's roots by driving the stake through them.

DEALING WITH A ROOT-BOUND PLANT

Occasionally, usually through neglect, a container-grown plant becomes root-bound. What this means is that the roots have overtaken the space available, and, without space in which to search for food, have started to wind round each other. Left to continue in this fashion, the plant will eventually choke to death, as the roots run out of nourishment. Root girdling, as it is known, can also render the plant unstable in windy conditions for the rest of its life.

You need to remove the plant from the container – at this stage probably by cutting the container away, if it is plastic, or by breaking it, if it is terracotta – and then start to tease out the roots as gently as possible, cutting cleanly those roots that are very tangled. The aim in doing this is to leave as much undamaged root surface as possible.

Plant out in the normal way, in a generous planting hole, with the roots spread out as much as you can. Give the plant plenty of water and nutrients.

BELOW *Take the plant out of its pot, if necessary by destroying the pot, and gently tease out the roots, removing any that are too tangled to tease out. Replant in a larger pot, then fill with compost and water the plant well. If necessary, trim the top growth of the plant a little.*

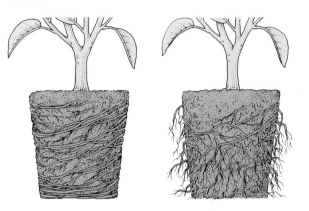

To root-prune, dig a trench around the shrub just wider than the circumference of its top growth. Cut off any thick, woody shoots and shorten them by about half. Put a barrier of slates or plastic sheeting around the base of the trench, and backfill the area, adding compost.

Eventually, you may well have to root-prune the plant again, if it becomes root-bound. This technique has proved very useful as a method of controlling over-vigorous fruit trees in small gardens and may be far more effective than pruning the shoots and stems of a plant.

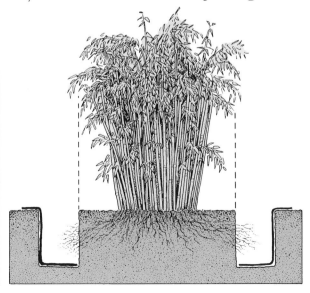

LEFT *Bamboo is notorious for spreading, and in a small garden, you may well have to contain its growth by root pruning. Dig out a trench, about 45cm (18in) deep, at the point where you wish to stop the plant from spreading, and cut off any roots that penetrate further than this. Line the trench with plastic sheeting and backfill with soil. You can also grow bamboo well in large containers.*

PROPAGATION FROM ROOTS

Roots do not merely provide the foundations and plumbing for the stems and leaves. They also have the potential to regenerate new plants from old. As a result, you can increase your stocks of plants by taking cuttings from the roots of certain plants (see below). Not all plants welcome having their roots disturbed, however, and some may die if they are moved, once they have become established. To retain the plant, your only solution is to take root cuttings from the parent plant and grow a new generation.

One such plant is the Californian poppy (*Romneya coulteri*). If you have to move it, lift the complete plant and take all the root cuttings you can, because if you put the plant back in the ground it will die. Once the cuttings have been made, they go straight into a flowerpot. *Romneya coulteri* is always grown in containers, because it really does resent being transplanted.

Cut each root into small pieces about 5cm (2in) long. To distinguish the base of the root from the crown end, make a straight cut at the crown end and an angled cut at the base (you need to do this to ensure that you do not plant the roots upside-down). Plant them in a layer of compost with the straight-cut end just level with the top of the compost. Cover with coarse grit and water regularly. When the cuttings have developed, pot them up into individual pots.

RIGHT *The Californian poppy,* Romneya coulteri, *hates to have its roots disturbed. If you need to move the plant, you will have to take root cuttings to ensure its survival.*

PLANTS PROPAGATED FROM ROOT CUTTINGS

Plants can be propagated from their roots, as well as from seeds and leaves, but not all plants like to have their roots disturbed. The following plants can be successfully propagated from root cuttings:

TREES
Ailanthus altissima
Mespilus germanica
Populus tremula
Prunus avium
Ulmus hollandica

SHRUBS
Aesculus parviflora
Romneya coulteri
Rosa nitida
Rubus cockburnianus
Sambucus canadensis

HERBACEOUS PERENNIALS
Acanthus spinosus
Anchusa azurea
Dicentra spectabilis
Gaillardia
Gypsophila paniculata
Papaver orientale
Phlox paniculata
Primula denticulata
Pulsatilla vulgaris
Trollius
Verbascum

CLIMBERS
Bignonia capreolata
Campsis radicans
Celastrus orbiculatus
Solanum crispum
Wisteria floribunda

ALPINES
Carduncellus rhaponticoides
Geranium dalmaticum
Morisia monanthos
Pulsatilla

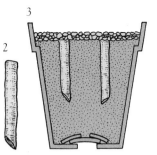
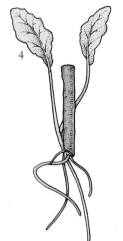

1 *Cut the root into pieces.*
2 *Make a straight cut at the top of the root and an oblique cut at the base.*
3 *Insert the root, base*

down, into a pot of cuttings compost. Cover with grit and keep moist.
4 *After a few weeks roots and leaves will develop.*

LEFT *When taking cuttings from roots, you need to be careful to mark the top and bottom of the root, since it needs to be inserted in the compost vertically, the right way up, with the stem end of the root at the top and the growing tip of the root at the base. The easiest way is to make a straight cut for the top of the root and an oblique cut for the base.*

HOW CUTTINGS FORM ROOTS

Propagation from cuttings is one of the most common methods of getting plants to reproduce themselves. There are three main types of cutting: stem, leaf and root. The aim of the first two (see page 78) is to persuade a part of the plant that has no roots to produce them – these are called adventitious roots. With root cuttings, the object is to persuade a root to form adventitious shoots.

Propagation by root cutting (see above) is one of the simplest, most foolproof ways of raising new plants, but how are stems persuaded to create roots?

Adventitious roots generally develop from the young cells produced by the cambium, the layer of cells responsible for thickening stems. Adventitious root growth is encouraged in the cutting by hormones known as auxins, which are produced naturally in the base of the cutting. Science has supplied us with synthetic auxins that we can apply to the base of the plant to encourage this natural root-making process. Rooting hormones can be bought in specific concentrations for softwood and hardwood cuttings, but care should be taken not to overdo the application, as it can harm the tissue. In the case of some plants that root easily, such as rosemary (*Rosmarinus officinalis*), rooting hormone will not be needed.

DIVIDING FIBROUS ROOTS

Plants with fibrous roots can be divided to form new plants, usually after flowering has finished. With small plants, lift them and divide the clump in half, using two hand forks back to back. With bigger clumps, use two garden forks back to back. For really tough fibrous roots, you may need to cut through the clump with a spade. Looser, more fleshy roots can sometimes be pulled apart by hand. Whichever method you use, try to avoid damaging the rootstock any more than is necessary.

PLANTS THAT DO NOT REQUIRE A ROOTING HORMONE
Buddleia cvs
Escallonia
Forsythia sp.
Lonicera (climber and bush)
Philadelphus sp.
Populus cvs and sp. (poplar)
Rosa rugosa cvs
Salix cvs and sp. (willow)
Spiraea cvs
Weigela sp.

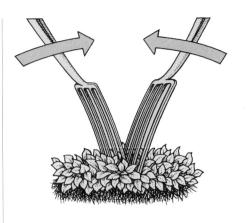

RIGHT *Many of the perennials with fibrous root systems can be propagated by division. In other words, when a clump gets large enough, you can break it into two smaller pieces. The easiest way with big clumps is to insert two forks, back to back, and put pressure on the forks to force the clump apart. Smaller clumps can be divided by digging them up carefully and then splitting them apart with your hands.*

Make decent-sized planting holes, with some compost at the base, place the plant in its new planting position and water well. Firm in around the plant.

DIVIDING RHIZOMATOUS PLANTS

Plants with thick rhizomes, such as *Iris* sp. and *Bergenia* sp., can be propagated by cutting the rhizomes into sections, provided that each section has a bud. Dust the cut areas with fungicide and, in the case of irises, trim the leaves to about 15cm (6in). Replant the rhizomes with the leaves and buds upright, close to the soil surface. Firm in and water.

SUCKERS

For most gardeners, sucker growths are the last sight they want to see. Many ornamental garden plants, such as hybrid roses, are grafted on to a vigorous rootstock. If a sucker originating from the rose rootstock is allowed to grow and compete with the grafted hybrid rose, eventually the hybrid rose will die, killed by the faster growth rate of the sucker. For this reason suckers *must* be removed as soon as they emerge.

BELOW Iris rhizomes can be propagated easily by splitting the rhizomes into pieces. Each piece must have a bud on it or it will not grow. Trim the leaves down to about 15cm (6in) and replant with the rhizomes half-buried. Firm in well and water.

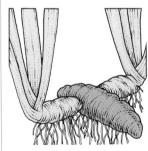

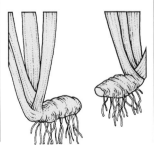

PLANTS PROPAGATED BY DIVISION

The following plants can be propagated by division:

Achillea	Helenium	Pulmonaria
Aconitum	Helianthus	Rheum
Astilbe	Helleborus orientalis	Rudbeckia
Astrantia	Hemerocallis	Salvia nemarosa
Bergenia	Hosta	Scabiosa caucasica
Coreopsis cordifolia	Iris (rhizomatous)	Sedum spectabile
Crambe cordifolia	Liatris	Solidago
Crocosmia	Lobelia cardinalis	Stachys byzantina
Epilobium	Lychnis	Symphytum
	Nepeta	Tradescantia
	Paeonia (with care)	Trollius
	Phormium	Veronica

UNDERGROUND STORAGE ORGANS

Bulbs, corms, rhizomes and tubers are all forms of underground storage for the plant. They have adapted so that they can withstand cold and/or drought, so that when the temperature warms up in spring, they can provide the energy for the plant to put on new growth.

BULBS

A bulb is, in fact, rather like a squashed shoot, compressed horizontally, with a central apical bud from which the new leaves eventually emerge. The outermost, scaly brown leaves of some bulbs – onions, tulips, daffodils – protect the plant from insect damage and soil microorganisms. Not all bulbs have this outer skin, however. In lilies, for example, the scales that are contained within a daffodil bulb are separate and attached to the basal plate of the bulb. They dry out more easily as a result, and are more likely to become damaged.

The bulb goes through a characteristic cycle of development, starting as a meristem and culminating in flowering and seed production. There are two stages – the first is vegetative, when leaves are produced, and the second reproductive, when flowers and seeds are produced.

Bulbs also reproduce themselves by producing offsets, or, in the case of the lily, by disintegrating into several bulblets. Contrary to what most gardeners believe, bulbs are not therefore all perennials. Daffodils are, and their flowers develop from axillary buds that form around the main part of the bulb, leaving the apical bud free to develop

BELOW LEFT The elements of a tulip bulb, which has an outer protective skin, showing the principal flowering stem (FAR LEFT) and the embryonic daughter bulbs (LEFT). The lily bulb (BELOW AND RIGHT) is a scaly bulb and has no outer covering, so the bulbs are relatively fragile.

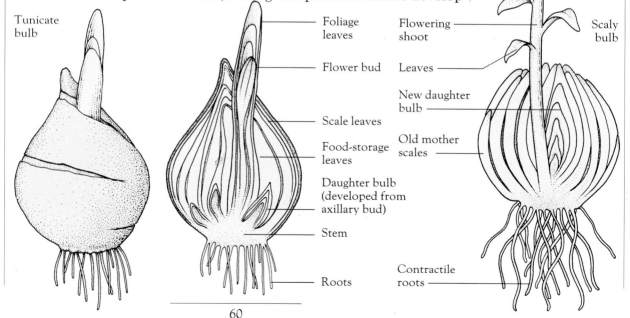

Tunicate bulb

Foliage leaves

Flower bud

Scale leaves

Food-storage leaves

Daughter bulb (developed from axillary bud)

Stem

Roots

Flowering shoot

Leaves

New daughter bulb

Old mother scales

Contractile roots

Scaly bulb

RIGHT *The giant lily (Cardiocrinum giganteum) is a striking six-footer with massive, scented creamy trumpets. Unfortunately the main bulb dies after flowering and it will be another five years before the offsets flower in their turn. It can also be propagated from seed, but that takes even longer – seven years before it flowers! When growing it from bulbs, plant them just below the soil surface in autumn, in rich, moist soil and in a partially shade site.*

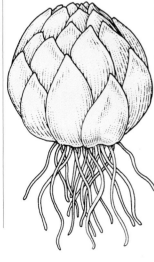

leaves. Tulips, however, are annual, with the flower being produced by the apical bud, and next year's leaves (and possibly its flowers) coming from new bulbs.

Bulbs also have the ability to form adventitious roots, from the bulb's flat stem. In some species these roots can contract, shortening and thickening, and serving to pull the bulb down to an appropriate depth in the soil for its protection. You can propagate bulbs by digging them up and separating the new bulblets from the main bulb. The scales of lily bulbs can be broken apart and, under moist, humid conditions, will produce one or more small bulbs at the base.

CORMS

A corm is the swollen base of a stem, which is enclosed by dry, scale-like leaves. Unlike bulbs, which are composed predominantly of leaf scales, the corm is a solid stem, with a covering – called a tunic – that prevents injury and water loss. At the apex of the corm is a terminal shoot that will develop into leaves and flowers, and in large corms there may be several of these. A corm has two types of root system: a fibrous one from the base, and enlarged, fleshy, contractile roots that work in the same way as they do for bulbs.

Like bulbs, corms produce small offsets called cormels, which can be used for propagation, although they have to reach an appropriate size before they will flower. Growth of leaves and flowers is at the expense of the corm's food reserves. After the flowers have formed, the corm develops a new corm above the old one, which withers away.

RHIZOMES

Yet another form of swollen stem – in this case a horizontal stem that runs just below the soil surface – is known as a rhizome (from the Greek *rhizoma*, meaning 'root', although, just to confuse you, it is not one). Roots and shoots develop from nodes on rhizomes, and as a result these plants will spread over quite a large area if left unchecked. They are easy to propagate, by cutting the rhizome into pieces. However, you do have to ensure that the part you wish to propagate bears the bud for a shoot.

TUBERS

A tuber is the swollen tip of a rhizome, and it displays similar characteristics, with axillary buds (eyes) that form new shoots. Once the buds develop into shoots, new adventitious roots and rhizomes form below

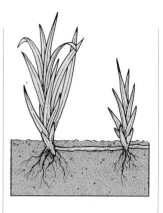

ABOVE *Iris rhizomes will spread quickly, as the buds on the rhizomes produce new plants, making it easy to divide up an iris bed that is getting old or overcrowded and to replant it elsewhere.*

RIGHT *A gladiolus corm showing the new corm developing on top of the old one, and the cormels produced around the base of the old corm. They can be split off and replanted in order to increase the stock of gladioli.*

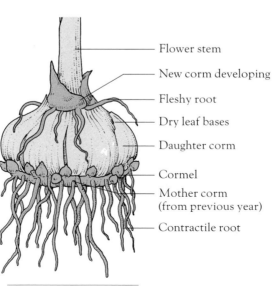

Flower stem

New corm developing

Fleshy root

Dry leaf bases

Daughter corm

Cormel

Mother corm (from previous year)

Contractile root

BELOW *Tubers have 'eyes' that develop new shoots. Like rhizomes, these can be split up, provided that each piece of tuber has an 'eye' from which a new plant can sprout.*

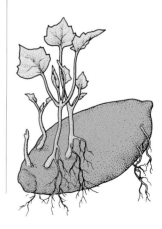

PLANTING POTATOES

Make a drill about 15cm (6in) deep. Plant maincrop potatoes about 40cm (15in) apart, with the eyes facing upwards. Make the rows about 75cm (30in) apart. New potatoes can be planted slightly closer together. Cover with soil.

When the plants are about (25cm) 10in high, earth up around each plant to prevent any potatoes near the surface from turning green.

Potatoes can also be grown under black plastic, to avoid the chore of earthing up. To plant this way, roll out a sheet of plastic and bury the sides. Make cross-shaped cuts the same distance apart as given above, and plant each potato through the cross, about 10cm (4in) deep.

Harvest potatoes as the flowers open. Potatoes can be stored in clamps (see below) for up to six months.

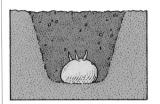

BELOW *Potatoes need to be planted well below the soil surface, and then earthed up (*RIGHT*) as the shoots develop.*

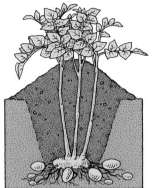

CLAMPING SWEDES
Make a layer of straw about 20cm (8in) thick and stack the swedes on top, in a pyramid, with their necks facing outwards. Cover with a layer of straw, and then a layer of soil. Swedes will last up to six months in clamps. Watch that mice do not eat them.

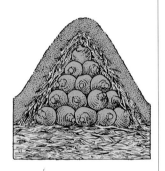

ROOT CROPS
Beetroot (*Beta vulgaris*)
Carrots (*Daucus carota*)
Jerusalem artichokes (*Helianthus tuberosus*)
Parsnips (*Pastinaca sativa*)
Potatoes (*Solanum tuberosum*)
Radishes (*Raphanus sativus*)
Scorzonera (*Scorzonera hispanica*)
Swedes (*Brassica napus*)
Sweet potatoes (*Ipomoea batatas*)
Turnips (*Brassica rapa*)

them, and so the process carries on, with the rhizomes eventually bearing new tubers. The old tubers are exhausted by the growth process and wither away, after bearing shoots and flowers.

ROOT TUBERS

Root tubers are the only form of storage organ, apart from tap roots, formed from actual roots. They operate in the same way as rhizome tubers, but they are actually formed from the root rather than from an underground stem.

ROOT VEGETABLES

What we are pleased to call root vegetables are not, in fact, all roots. Some – such as potatoes, sweet potatoes and Jerusalem artichokes – are tubers, but, in terms of planning the vegetable garden, they can all be classified as root crops.

One of the greatest benefits of root crops is that they can be stored. Being storage organs for the plant, they naturally keep well. There are two main methods of storing root vegetables: in layers of sand (as for carrots), or in clamps or boxes in the dark. Light is the chief enemy of most root crops, which is why potatoes have to be earthed up or covered in black plastic. Failure to do so will result in the tubers developing green colouring, which is not only unpalatable but can be toxic.

CHAPTER THREE

THE GREEN MACHINE

Plants, with their ability to make food from simple inorganic compounds, are essential to all forms of life. They are at the base of all food chains – the suppliers of the oxygen that is vital to animal life.

After a long period of dormancy in winter, plants start to unfurl their leaves as the temperature and light levels increase in spring. Although many plants are grown for the beauty of their leaves alone, these leaves are, in fact, a vital power house for the plant. They operate like solar panels, harvesting the sunlight to make sugar and starches

Plants adapt to their circumstances. The giant Lobelia keniensis (LEFT) *from Mount Kenya has a rosette of leaves that acts as a water-catcher; low-growing woodland plants, like bluebells* (BELOW), *come into flower before the tree canopy cuts light out.*

into chlorophyll – the green pigment that extracts carbon dioxide and water from the atmosphere and converts it into energy. This process is known as photosynthesis.

The chemical changes involved in photosynthesis can be slowed down or speeded up, depending on the amount of any one of the factors necessary to effect this change. For example, when sunlight levels fall, the process of photosynthesis slows down or stops. If the plant is prevented from reaching one of the sources essential for photosynthesis, it will compensate by devising a means of doing so. It will naturally try to find the light, its questing shoots bending towards whatever source of light it can find. Cells will grow faster on the shadier side of the plant, to bend the shoot towards the light, in an attempt to obtain an equal spread of light all round the plant.

Plants that are grown in low light levels tend to produce large leaves, as they desperately seek to increase the 'solar panels' provided by the leaves, in an attempt to increase sugar production. Lots of stored sugar energy tends, on the other hand, to produce a mass of flowers.

Plants are also affected by the timing of the light source, and they have adapted gradually to different levels of light in different parts of the world. Plants usually put on their greatest growth spurt when daylight hours start to lengthen, and they close down (to dormancy) when light levels diminish.

As a result of these different forms of adaptation, the gardener needs to consider the conditions required by the plants he has chosen to grow, since they may well come from parts of the world where temperature and light levels vary enormously. Too much hot sun will scorch leaves that have adapted to a cooler, moister atmosphere; too little light may prevent a plant from flowering at all.

Precisely because the gardener interferes with nature by choosing what he wishes to grow, rather than by letting nature herself decide (as should occur in a truly wild garden), he will need to help the plant to perform this balancing act by supplying the correct ingredients, at the right times. It is no good showering the plant with water in the dormant season, when it has shut up shop for the winter; or deciding to move the plant from one place in the garden to another when all its energy is being spent in trying to convert sunlight into food. In the first instance, the plant will receive no benefit; in the second, it will be unable to cope and will wither or die.

Once you understand a little about the way the plant actually functions, you begin to realize that the dos and don'ts contained in gardening books are not simply a set of rigid rules but are, on the whole, ways of improving the plant's chances of survival.

Since plants are not cheap to buy as container-grown specimens, and few people have the time, energy or space to raise many plants from

HOW PHOTOSYNTHESIS WORKS

The process of photosynthesis can be clearly seen by observing water plants such as the Canadian pond-weed (*Elodea crispa*). If you put it under a microscope, its individual cellular organs – or chloroplasts – can be seen at the points where the green pigment is concentrated. The chloroplasts absorb molecules of carbon dioxide and water, and the energy provided by sunlight splits the water molecules into their component atoms of hydrogen and oxygen. When the hydrogen and carbon dioxide combine to form simple sugars, like glucose, oxygen is given off as a by-product. With an underwater plant like *Elodea*, you can actually see the bubbles of oxygen rising to the surface. The lighter and warmer the conditions, the faster the plant responds. But at night the production line in the leaves slows and finally shuts down altogether, starting up again the following morning.

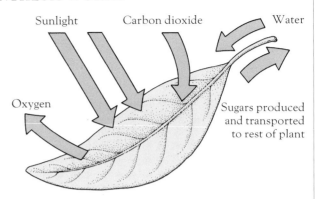

ABOVE *The processes that occur in a a leaf during photosynthesis, in which sunlight and carbon dioxide are absorbed from the atmosphere and turned into sugars, and water and oxygen are transpired through the pores.*

seed cuttings, creating the appropriate conditions to ensure the survival of those that you do buy makes economic sense. After all, why spend good money on a plant at the garden centre and then damage, or perhaps even kill, it by failing to provide the conditions it needs in order to flourish?

DORMANCY

A plant's growth and development are affected by seasonal changes. For thousands of years variations in day length have remained constant, and in temperate climates the timing of the colder season is more or less regular. Plants have learned to adapt to these conditions to ensure their successful survival.

During the winter, the plant's activity – both in storing energy and in growing – winds down almost to a standstill, but the plants still need this cold period in order to produce the hormone that eventually kick-starts growth when the temperature and daylight hours increase in the spring. This essential exposure to cold, in order to spring into growth, can be demonstrated by tulips.

Tulip bulbs must experience a drop in temperature to about 10°C (50°F) for 13–14 weeks in order for their flower buds to develop fully. If grown in warmer climates, tulips have to be dug up and refrigerated after flowering, or they will fail to flower the following year. Onions grown for their bulbs can be prevented from flowering by keeping the bulbs at warm temperatures throughout the year. Many seeds also have to go through a cold spell in order to germinate (see page 104).

LEAVES

The leaves of plants are constructed to exploit their environment as fully as possible. Since their primary function is to capture light for the purpose of photosynthesis, nature has ensured that they are arranged in ways that make this possible. The stalk by which the leaf is attached to the main stem – the petiole – is deliberately flexible, so that the leaf can rotate, if necessary, to take advantage of the sun's rays. However, some leaves (known as sessile, rather than petiole, leaves) are attached directly to the stem.

To gain the maximum benefit from the light, the plant's meristem ensures that the leaves are arranged around the stem, so that each leaf gets as much light as possible. There are three principal leaf arrangements – alternate, opposite and whorled (see right). In most plants, pairs of leaves, and each alternate leaf, point in different directions down the stem, to give it the best chance of catching the light.

Each leaf has a complex vascular (vessel) or circulation system, through which fluids are transported to and from the leaf's surface, and these vein patterns are as distinctive as the leaf shapes themselves.

RIGHT Leaves are arranged on the plant to allow maximum exposure to sunlight, in order to increase the rate of photosynthesis. The three arrangements shown here are just an example of the different ways in which leaves gain exposure to the light.

LEAF AND STEM SHAPES

There is a wide range of leaf and stem shapes, both in the construction of the leaf – from a simple single leaf to a highly compound form (see below) – and in the form that its margins take, although botanists do not yet know how, or why, some of these adaptations have developed. These differences of leaf shape and form help botanists to classify plants into groups and are often used by them to help to describe plants:

MACROPHYLLA large leaves, e.g. *Quercus macrophylla*
MICROPHYLLA small leaves, e.g. *Cotoneaster microphyllus*
RUGOSE wrinkled or rough leaves, e.g. *Rosa rugosa*
TOMENTOSE leaves covered in dense hairs, e.g. *Cerastium tomentosum*

LEFT Leaves vary in shape from the least complex (simple) to the most complex (compound).

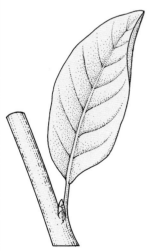

Simple petiole leaf

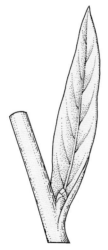

Sessile leaf

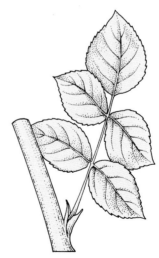

Compound leaf

STOMATA

The surface of a plant leaf is covered by a layer of cells known as the epidermis, which is in turn covered by a waterproof material. In some plants (those adapted to hot conditions) this outer layer is thicker than in others, and possibly covered by a waxy substance or by hairs, to slow down water loss. In the green parts of the plant involved in photosynthesis, the epidermis contains pores, called stomata, through which the gases used in the process enter the leaf and through which water also evaporates. These stomata work like valves, opening and closing

Alternate

Opposite

Whorled

RIGHT *The leaves of ivy, in this case* Hedera colchica *'Dentata Variegata', which will grow happily even in shade, are arranged like tiles on a roof, so that each one receives maximum exposure to whatever light is available.*

WHY NOT WATER PLANTS IN SUNSHINE?

You are sometimes told that you must not water plants when the sun is on them, but the reason may have escaped you. The answer is twofold: first, the delicate valve mechanism of the stomata has adapted to hot, sunny conditions, and by suddenly drenching the plant with water you confuse the mechanism, with resulting adverse effects on the plant. If the leaves are drenched with water, the stomata respond very rapidly and open, but as the air around the leaf dries, the stomata rapidly close, which can cause stress to the plant. To avoid leaf damage the propagator must be capable of maintaining a high humidity around the leaf and thus reduce stress to a minimum.

Second, small drops of water falling on the leaves act rather like a magnifying glass, through which the sun's rays pass and can burn the leaves, rather in the same way that you can set light to a piece of paper held under a magnifying glass in the sun's path.

according to the external conditions. In most plants, the stomata are open in the daylight, when photosynthesis is taking place, and closed at night, when it stops. If the plant is losing too much water through evaporation, its stomata will close and reduce moisture loss until the roots can make up for the lack of water in the plant's main channels. But while the stomata are closed, photosynthesis cannot take place. A plant that is losing too much water therefore becomes distressed and concentrates all its energy on retaining its water balance. So plants deprived of the necessary quantities of water will not grow as well as those that are watered regularly.

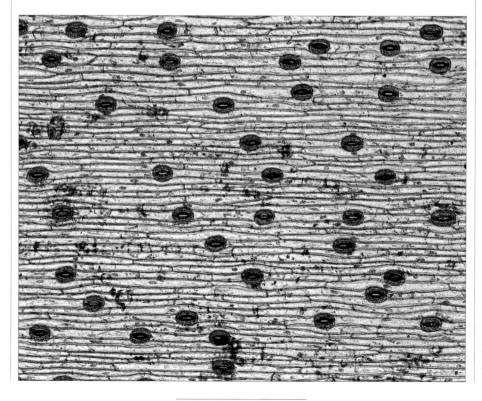

LEFT A close-up of the stomata on a hyacinth leaf. There are literally thousands of pores on the surface of some leaves, particularly those adapted to low light levels.

WATER AND THE PLANT

It may come as a surprise to most gardeners to find out just how much water a plant actually needs to survive. Of all the rain that falls on a garden, almost two-thirds is promptly recycled by the plants, in a process known as transpiration. The plant draws up the moisture from the soil through its roots and then pumps it upwards to the leaves, where it evaporates.

The process of transpiration may seem wasteful but in fact it is essential for the plant. First, the water is used to carry minerals and nutrients from the soil to the plant's uppermost leaves; second, the transpired water helps to cool down the leaves. Water vapour escaping from a warm, moist object carries heat away with it, allowing the

WATERING TECHNIQUES

The main aim when watering is to provide an adequate supply of water to penetrate deep enough into the soil to furnish the roots with moisture. Consistent light watering will simply encourage surface rooting at the expense of deeper roots, and the surface roots will be more vulnerable to drought. Small quantities of water will quickly evaporate from the soil surface, before the water has had a chance to reach the roots of the plants.

If you dig a small hole in the soil after watering, you may well be surprised to see that the water has barely penetrated the surface. The solution is to allow the first soaking of water to penetrate and then give a second application shortly afterwards.

Plants with deep roots may benefit from having a pipe inserted near their base, which will help to carry the water down to lower levels. Or bury a pot with a drainage hole in the bottom near the plant, and fill that with water.

The plant's water requirements depend partly on where it comes from – desert, forest, mountain or valley. However, all plants need far less water during the dormant season and far greater quantities during the growing season, especially if fruit and vegetable crops are to swell and ripen.

All newly planted and transplanted plants, and seedlings, need plenty of moisture at regular intervals, until their roots become sufficiently well established to draw water from the soil. Mulching the soil (see page 37) will help to cut down on moisture loss.

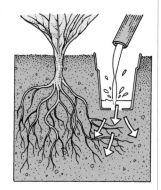

RIGHT *To enable water to reach the deeper roots of certain plants, it may be a good idea to insert a pipe or pot with a drainage hole close by, which can then be filled with water. This ensures that the water reaches a point where the roots are able to take up the moisture.*

REVIVING A WILTED CONTAINER PLANT

Provided that a plant has wilted through lack of water, rather than as a result of disease, it can often be revived. If the pot feels exceptionally light, then almost certainly the compost has dried out. You can resuscitate the plant – provided the leaves are still green, even if wilted – by immersing it, in its pot, in a bucket of water. Leave it there until bubbles stop rising to the surface, which indicates that the compost has fully absorbed the maximum amount of water. The plant should then be removed from the bucket to allow excess water to drain away and to restore the water and oxygen balance in the compost.

LEFT *This* Sequoia giganteum, *photographed in the Sequoia National Park in California, is the world's largest living tree. Sequoias are also among the oldest trees and transpire literally hundreds of gallons of water an hour.*

surface of the leaf to cool, much in the same way that we cool down when we perspire.

While it is not really difficult to imagine how water travels from the roots of a small plant to the tips of its leaves, when you look at a large tree, such as the Californian redwood (*Sequoia sempervirens*), which can easily reach 90m (300ft) in its natural habitat, you do wonder how the water gets from the soil to the topmost branches.

In fact, inside the tree there are continuous moving columns of water, as the roots suck up the moisture from the soil and the leaves transpire it out through their pores. The process of transpiration creates a sort of suction, which helps to keep the columns of water full. Roots also have the ability to exert a certain amount of pressure, which is needed to help to force the water up the trunk. In particularly dry conditions, this pressure becomes very important, because it helps to push water up from below and to keep the columns intact, even when the transpiration rate from the leaves is very high.

The diameter of a tree actually changes as the levels of water within it rise and fall. The diameter reduces slightly during the day, when the leaves are losing most water, and increases again at night, when transpiration slows down.

The quantities of water lost in transpiration are truly astonishing. A 15m (50ft) tree can lose up to 220 litres (48 gallons) per hour, and each acre (0.4ha) of broad-leaved woodland in Britain transpires 30,000 litres (6,600 gallons) a day. A tomato plant will suck up 115 litres (25 gallons) of water during its growing season.

The plant transpires such a large quantity of water for two reasons: it needs water to fulfil the process of photosynthesis, and the pores on the leaves will open only if the plant is 'full' of water.

When you realize how much water a plant uses up, you begin to understand why drought causes it to wilt. When this happens, the water columns inside the plant break and vacuums are formed in the conducting vessels, and so the plant loses rigidity. During such stressed conditions, the stomata in the leaves close to allow the plant to conserve water. Once the moisture again becomes available to the roots, the water columns build up and the plant recovers.

Some plants have evolved to survive in local environmental conditions in various ways. Desert plants, for example, close the stomata in their leaves during the day and open them at night.

RIGHT *Plants have devised different ways of retaining water. Sedums are among a group of plants with tough, leathery surfaces to their leaves, which are arranged in rosettes to enable them to catch the water, and whose leaf tissue is largely composed of water.*

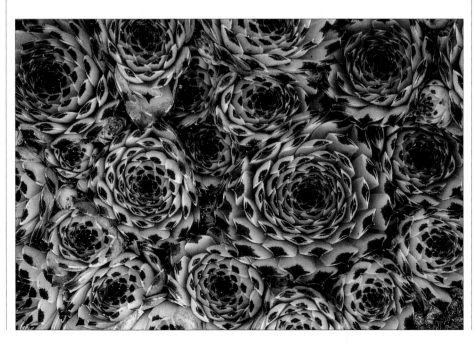

STEMS

The stem of the plant serves several purposes. It provides the means by which liquids are transported from the roots to the leaves, and vice versa; it raises the plants to the light; and, in the case of woody plants, it also provides a supporting structure for the canopy of leaves above.

The flow of liquids up and down the plant is conducted by means of separate bundles of vessels contained within the stem – the plumbing of the plant (see diagram below). Each vascular (vessel) bundle contains both xylem and phloem – the xylem vessels take the nutrient solution from the roots to the leaves, and the phloem carry the downward movement of food in solution. These vessels are separated in woody-stemmed plants by a layer known as the cambium (see below), and are protected on the outside by the bark.

GRAFTING

If you wish to combine the best characteristics of two plants, grafting is the method by which this is achieved. It involves the permanent union

---

CAMBIUM

If you stripped the bark off a woody plant, you would find just beneath it the glistening cambial region. The cambium layer of cells in the stem of a plant divide laterally and are the means by which the stems of woody plants increase in diameter. In many perennials, it is the activity in the cambial cells that turns the plant from a herbaceous to a woody one. It is also the means by which new xylem is produced on the inside of the cambium and phloem on the outside (see diagram).

On a woody plant, an outer layer of cork replaces the epidermis found in softer plants. This cork layer, which is several cell layers thick, increases laterally. Its surface layer comprises the bark of the tree, whose colour and pattern are an important feature.

The healing of wounds is made possible by the fact that living cells surrounding the damaged area have the ability to form healing tissue, called callus. When damage occurs to the branches or surface bark of trees, an increase in plant hormone concentration takes place in the undamaged cells surrounding the wound. This activity stimulates the cambium cells to divide and form a layer of cells (callus) over the wounded area. At first this tissue is soft, later taking on a corky texture, before finally becoming hard and woody. With large wounds it may take several years before the exposed area is totally covered with callus.

BELOW A cross-section through the stem of a woody plant showing the cambial region.

Cortex
Epidermis
Xylem
Cambium
Phloem

MAKING A WHIP-AND-TONGUE GRAFT

There are several methods of grafting. Whip-and-tongue is one of the more commonly used.

Select a suitable rootstock that has been growing for at least a year. Trim the base stem of the rootstock of all branches, and make a sloping cut, about 4cm (1½in) long, in the top.

Make a shallow slice in the cut surface of the rootstock and a matching cut in the scion.

Cut off a vigorous hardwood stem from the chosen scion. Make a top cut in the scion just above a bud, about four buds up from the base. Then make a base cut the same length as that of the rootstock, just below the bottom bud.

Attach the scion to the rootstock, so that the cut surfaces align exactly. Bind them with clear polythene tape. The tape can be removed once the cut surfaces form a callus.

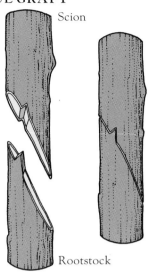

Scion

Rootstock

---

of a stem or bud from one plant with the rootstock of another plant. Grafting can only be carried out between closely related plants. Rather like organ transplants in humans, there must be a degree of compatibility for the transplant to 'take' and form a successful union.

In grafting, the base of the shoot, called the 'scion', is shaped and inserted into an incision in the stem or branch of a rooted plant, called the 'stock'. It is absolutely vital that there is good contact between the soft tissues of both scion and stock. Normally, once the union has been made, the two parts are bound tightly together to keep the contact close, and the graft – as it is known – is often covered with wax or bandaged with polythene tape to ensure that the join does not dry out before the two tissues unite.

Another form of grafting, called budding, is the same process in essence, but a small axillary bud is used rather than a stem. This bud has a small portion of the outer tissues of the stem attached to it. Although there are many forms of incision – depending on the type of stock and scion being grafted and the way they fit together – the principle is the same for all of them.

Success in grafting depends on good, clean cuts, matching the surfaces without delay, and ensuring that the cut surfaces do not dry out. The object of grafting is to get the maximum area of cambium in contact, since this is where the new cells are going to form.

Because the plant is, literally, wounded in the process, there is a danger of infection, so all grafting has to be made as sterile as possible, using clean, sharp equipment.

Once the graft has taken, the old stock can be cut back to just above the new shoot that develops from the grafted scion.

With any grafted plant you will get an exact replica of the plant from which you took the scion. So if you had a hybrid apple, for example, which would not breed true to type from seed or which was even sterile, you could nevertheless produce its identical twin by grafting a scion from it on to the stock of another apple tree. Among the various reasons for grafting are: to combine the benefits of different plants, and to find a solution to particular inherent weaknesses. In fruit trees, certain rootstocks have been developed to control the size and fruiting capacity of specific trees, to increase resistance to pests and diseases, or to increase tolerance to particular soil conditions. Another reason for grafting is that it may take fifteen years for a tree to fruit, but by grafting it on to a suitable rootstock you can start to get fruit within five years; this is obviously of great value to commercial growers.

One further major advantage of grafting is that more than one scion can be attached to the rootstock, thereby creating, say, a family fruit tree bearing several varieties of apple. This has two benefits: first, it may help to overcome the problem that some trees (such as most pears, for example) cannot be pollinated unless there is a compatible tree nearby; second, in small gardens you are able to produce several varieties within a limited area.

PLANTS WITH ORNAMENTAL BARK

Trees
Acer griseum
A. grosseri
Betula papyrifera
Carpinus betulus
Parrotia persica
Platanus × hispanica
Prunus maackii
P. serrula
Salix daphnoides

Shrubs
Cornus alba cvs
Euonymus alatus
Kerria japonica
Leycesteria formosa
Rhododendron barbatum
Rosa roxburghii
Rubus cockburnianus
R. thibetanus
Salix irrorata

PROPAGATING FROM LEAVES AND STEMS

RIGHT *When taking a soft cutting, the lower leaves should be removed before dipping the base of the stem in rooting hormone. Then insert it in the cuttings compost, watering well and enclosing it in a transparent polythene bag.*

Various parts of the plant can be used for propagation (see pages 56 and 79–81), but stems, and less commonly leaves, are used in a range of genera.

Quite a few of the more attractive house plants will reproduce themselves from cuttings taken from their leaves, among them *Coleus, Saintpaulia, Begonia rex* and *Streptocarpus* (see page 80). With another house plant, *Kalanchoe*, an even easier method of propagation has developed. Miniature plants are carried in the notches along the leaf margins, and these simply drop off and, with luck, plant themselves, to form another generation of *Kalanchoe*.

The advantage of any form of cutting is that it will be an exact replica of the parent plant (botanists refer to them as clones), because no cross-fertilization, such as that which occurs in seed formation (see page 94), has taken place.

The most common form of propagation is from the stems of plants, because, as we have already seen on page 74, the wound-healing or callus-forming properties of the plant create tissue from which adventitious roots will grow, given the right circumstances.

There are various types of stem cutting, depending on the type of plant – soft, semi-ripe or hardwood. Soft cuttings are taken from the tips of soft green shoots, and are usually taken in spring or summer. They are vulnerable to water loss and need plenty of moisture, usually being placed in a mist propagator or a plastic bag. Semi-ripe cuttings are taken from a wide range of shrubs after flowering, and consist of a shoot with the heel of the main stem attached. These can be rooted outside, provided they are given some shelter. Ripe and hardwood cuttings can be taken in autumn and, in most cases, left outside to root at their leisure, although a few will not do so.

With all cuttings the aim is to encourage the callus – the injury caused when the cutting is removed from the parent – to grow adventitious roots (see page 58). In the meantime, the plant needs moisture of some description, hence the benefits of mist propagation. Even this is not without its drawbacks, however, since waterlogging will simply cause the cutting to rot, which means that the frequency at which the mist is applied is a critical factor.

Another cause of the premature demise of cuttings is impatience on the part of the propagator, who gets fed up waiting for something to happen and pulls up the cutting to inspect it. When the cutting has rooted, there will be signs of new leaf shoots. Until then, leave it alone.

PLANTS PROPAGATED BY STEM CUTTINGS

Hardwood
Buddleia cvs
Forsythia sp.
Lonicera (climber and bush)
Philadelphus sp.
Populus cvs and sp. (Poplar)
Rosa rugosa cvs
Salix cvs and sp. (Willow)
Spiraea cvs
Weigela sp.

Semi-ripe
Chamaecyparis lawsoniana cvs
Escallonia sp.
Juniperus cvs
Olearia sp.
Passiflora cvs

Softwood
Alyssum saxitale
Aster novi-belgii cvs
Chrysanthemum cvs
Fuchsia cvs
Pelargonium cvs

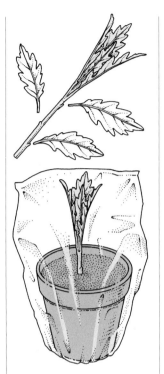

The procedure below explains how to take a soft cutting; semi-ripe cuttings are treated in the same way, but a heel of the main stem is taken with the cutting.

STEM CUTTINGS

Taking a soft cutting Choose a young, healthy side shoot in midsummer, after the plant has flowered.

Remove the lower leaves and dip the base in rooting powder. Insert it in a pot of sand and compost, water well and enclose in a transparent bag. Open this daily for one hour to allow fresh air in.

Layering a plant Some shrubs – such as cultivars, which will not grow true from seed – are better propagated by layering. You take a young shoot and a sharp knife or blade, and select a node on the stem. Carefully cut away the shoots from the node and then take a thin slice from the bark of the shoot, to expose the cambium layer. Put a bucketful of compost/sand/garden soil mixed together and peg down the shoot on top of it, making sure the cambium is in good contact with the soil. Serpentine layering – with several cuts in the stem, making several new plants – can be done on some climbing plants. Tip layering, in which the tip of a young shoot is pegged down, is done on brambles.

RIGHT *Layering a plant. A number of shrubs and some perennials, such as pinks and carnations, can be propagated by layering. This involves making a small nick in the stem of the plant, or removing a sliver of bark in the case of a shrub, and pegging down the shoot of the plant in good compost. The wounded part of the stem, in contact with the soil, will make adventitious roots, and eventually you will be able to cut off the tip, complete with roots.*

 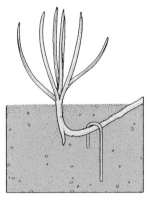 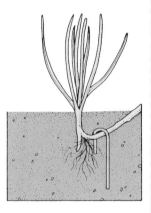

PLANTS PROPAGATED BY LAYERING

Serpentine layering	*Enkianthus campanulatus*	**Tip layering**
Celastrus scandens	*Hamamelis mollis* cvs	*Chlorophytum comosum*
Clematis sp.	*Magnolia* × *soulangiana*	'Variegatum'
Lapageria rosea	cvs	Most *Rubus* species and
Vitis cvs	*Parrotiopsis jacquemontia*	cultivars including:
Wisteria cvs	*Rhododendron* sp.	Blackberries
	Schizophragma	Loganberries
Simple layering	*hydrangeoides*	*Rubus cockburnianus*
Amelanchier sp.	*Syringa vulgaris* cvs	*R. thibetanus*
Chimonanthus praecox	*Tilia* × *euchlora*	*R.* × 'Tridel'

LEAF CUTTINGS

These should be made from mature, but still young, leaves, which are complete, normal and undamaged. Most plants suitable for leaf cuttings are indoor plants, so you can take the cuttings more or less throughout the year, although root development will tend to be slower in winter.

Drying out is the single biggest problem affecting leaf cuttings, so you need to enclose the propagation area within glass or polythene, and ensure that it is well watered.

Leaf petiole cuttings Some plants, such as begonias (other than *Begonia rex*), *Peperomia caperata* and *P. metallica*, and African violets (*Saintpaulia* sp.) can be propagated in this way.

Remove an undamaged leaf from the plant near the base. Cut through the leaf stalk (petiole) vertically, and insert the stalk in the compost. Gently firm the compost around the cutting, water and cover. Apply liquid feed when the new plantlets develop around the leaf petiole. Once the plants are big enough to be handled, you should pot them on.

Some plants, such as *Streptocarpus*, *Gloxinia* and *Gesneria* can be propagated from mid-rib leaf cuttings or, alternatively, from lateral vein (butterfly) cuttings.

PLANTS PROPAGATED BY LEAF CUTTINGS

Leaf petiole
Morisia monanthos
Peperomia cvs and sp.
Saintpaulia cvs
Sedum spectabile

Leaf sections
Begonia rex
B. masoniana
Sansevieria trifasciata
Sinningia speciosa
Streptocarpus cvs

LEAF PETIOLE CUTTINGS
These can be made from some indoor plants, simply by means of inserting the stem of the leaf into cuttings compost.

Leaf petiole cuttings

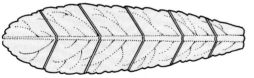

BUTTERFLY AND MID-RIB CUTTINGS
Certain house plants can be propagated by using sections of the leaf for propagation. In butterfly cuttings, the leaf is cut transversely into sections, with as many veins as possible in contact with the compost. In mid-rib cuttings, the veins on

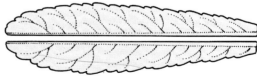

either side of the mid-rib are severed, and these will, when in contact with the soil, produce roots, stems and leaves, which can then be separated off into new plantlets.

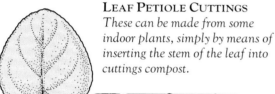

Butterfly cuttings

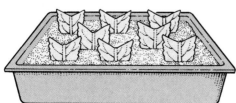

Mid-rib cuttings

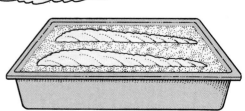

RIGHT *The handsomely coloured leaves of the flame nettle,* Coleus *(now officially* Solenostemon *sp.). These plants are normally propagated by seed, or by tip cuttings taken in summer.*

BELOW Kalanchoe, *on the other hand, produces its own plantlets along the margins of its leaves.*

Mid-rib cuttings First choose a good, healthy leaf. Then run a sharp knife along both sides of the mid-rib of the leaf, separating the leaf blade from it. This action of cutting the veins triggers the plant's response to wounding and the healing cells, called callus, then have the potential to produce all the different tissues that a new plant will need – root, stem and leaf.

Butterfly cuttings With butterfly cuttings the aim is to get as many of the leaf veins as you can in contact with the compost. You therefore cut across the leaf in sections that resemble butterfly wings, and then insert these upright in the soil. Water regularly and in time you will be rewarded with young plantlets at each vein point, which you can gently remove and then plant up in their own pots.

AUTUMN COLOUR

In broad-leaved woodlands, autumn matches spring in its myriad shades of foliage, except that the autumn tints are more various and more subtle. At this time of year, nature starts to recycle the resources from the summer's growth, closing down the upper levels of the plant and storing food as best she can for winter. In the temperate world plants do not judge the onset of winter by the fall in temperature so much as by the lowering of light levels. The trigger for the winter close-down is decreasing day length. Many of the crucial events in a plant's life are governed by day length (see page 114).

THE COLOUR CHANGE

In America, autumn is called the fall – and a very apt term it is. The autumn colour change in North America is so pronounced that it can be seen from space. The colour front marches southwards towards the tropics at the rate of 60–70km (37–43 miles) a day, so that in a matter of three weeks, around 300 million tons of chlorophyll are destroyed.

In some trees, the change from green to autumn colour is slow and subtle. The beech tree (*Fagus sylvatica*), common in English woodlands, changes slowly from green to yellow to brown. But what causes this colour change? The answer is the pigment, or lack of it, in the leaves. As sunlight levels fall, so the green parts of the leaf die, and what you then see in the leaf, giving it its autumn colour, are the other pigments, particularly carotene (which is, incidentally, also the cause of the orange colour of carrot roots). Carotene is not as efficient as chlorophyll at processing light and, when it too fails, the leaf dies altogether, falling off the tree.

Not all trees contain the same quantities of pigment, hence the difference in autumn leaf colour. The leaves of plants contain various forms of photosynthetic pigment, the principal one being chlorophyll, which is green. In addition to carotene, there are several other pigments, called xanthrophylls, which range in colour from yellow to colourless. A purplish-red pigment, known as anthocyanin, is present in some species of plants, and this is responsible for the dark red leaves of some Japanese maples and for the wonderful mahogany colour of copper beech.

Take the Japanese maple, *Acer palmatum*. Not only does the leaf colour vary between species, but it varies within the same species as well. Some will turn a magnificent scarlet, others a rather dull gold or brown. You will get a truly scarlet form on only about one in every hundred plants.

PLANTS FOR AUTUMN COLOUR

Climbers
Ampelopsis aconitifolia
Celastrus orbiculatus
Parthenocissus
   tricuspidata
Tropaeolum tuberosum
Vitis coignetiae

Trees
Acer platanoides
   'Cleveland'
Betula alleghanensis
Cercidiphyllum
   japonicum
Crateagus mollis

Fraxinus excelsior
   'Jaspidea'
Liquidambar styraciflua
Nyssa sylvatica
Parrotia persica
Prunus sargentii
Quercus rubra 'Aurea'
Sorbus americana
Toona sinensis

Shrubs
Acer palmatum
Berberis dictophylla
Corylopsis veitchiana
Enkianthus chinensis

Fothergilla major
Hamamelis virginiana
Lindera glauca
Ptelea trifoliata
Rosa rugosa
Sorbaria aitchisonii
Viburnum plicatum cvs
Zanthophyllum piperitum

Conifers
Ginkgo biloba
Larix lyallii
Metasequoia
Pseudolarix amabilis
Taxodium distichum

HOW DO THE LEAVES ACTUALLY FALL?

The leaves are attached to the tree in such a way that where they join the stem, there is a point of weakness, known as the abscission layer. On a horse chestnut (*Aesculus hippocastanum*), when the leaf is pulled away from the stem, you can see what appear to be marks like nails in a horse's hoof, which indicate where the vessels in the leaf joined those in the stem.

AUTUMN COLOUR VARIATION

Why are there better autumn colours some years than others? This occurs when the speed at which food is being manufactured by the plant exceeds the rate at which the food is being removed or used. This state of affairs can be brought about in several ways, of which the most common is too little water or insufficient nitrogen in the soil.

Red-leaved species, like the Japanese maple (*Acer palmatum* 'Atropurpureum') or *Rhus cotinus*, are grown chiefly for their coloured leaves, which contain anthocyanin. They tend to have the most intense red colour in a dry autumn, but if you feed them with too much nitrogenous manure you are apt to get the opposite effect. In autumn, the accumulation of sugars, and heightened coloration, are usually a consequence of continued food formation at a time when the sugars are not being removed as quickly and are not being used for growth.

So when you get sunny days with a lot of food production followed by cold nights, you will see very good colour in the leaves, since the sunny days increase the manufacture of sugars and the cold nights check their removal, and also check the absorption rate of nitrogen. Because the chlorophyll has to be disintegrated by sunlight, in order to

achieve any kind of brilliant coloration, trees and shrubs will give much better autumn colour when grown in full sunlight than when grown in partially shaded positions. You will also find that the south side of a tree or shrub is better coloured than the north side, and that you tend to get a faster change of colour and a more intense one in periods of drought.

ABOVE *The horse chestnut (Aesculus sp.) turns a golden-yellow in autumn as chlorophyll levels reduce, until the leaf shrivels up and falls off the tree.*

HOW PLANTS ADAPT

BELOW *Leaves have adapted in many ways to cope with varying climates and conditions. Palm fronds, being much divided, lose less water than a large expanse of soft green leaf, and therefore adapt well to hot, dry conditions.*

One point you quickly establish as a gardener is that not all of your plants require the same quantities of water or light in order to thrive. In periods of drought, some plants will appear to be perfectly happy, while others rapidly shrivel up and die. Why should this be so? The answer is adaptation. Some plants have evolved to live with different quantities and timings of water, and their cell structure has adapted over the millennia to cope with these fluctuations.

The most obvious form of adaptation is in leaf type. A quick look round the garden will reveal as many different leaf sizes and forms as there are plants: large, small, divided, glossy, felted, hairy, spiny,

needle-like, tough, soft. To some extent, when you know a little about leaf adaptation, you can work out from looking at a plant the kind of conditions that it requires, particularly when you know what botanical function the leaf is performing.

As we have seen, leaves are the means of capturing sunlight through the pigment of chlorophyll that they contain. Therefore in shady areas two characteristics are likely to be necessary – large leaf surfaces and very green leaves. Lack of sunlight is also going to mean that the leaves are unlikely to scorch, so they need less surface protection from the sun's rays.

Plants that grow in the Mediterranean regions of the world, on the other hand, with limited water supplies and strong sunlight to contend with, are often small or finely divided, and they may well be coated in various ways to prevent water loss – either with soft hairs or with a waxy covering.

Cacti, living in regions where the climate is extreme, have some of the most interesting leaf adaptations. Much depends on their making the most of the very infrequent but often copious rain showers, the blistering heat and the animals searching out plants as the only source of water. So what does nature produce? Plants with prickly or spiny leaves, often in a rosette shape that funnels water into a central reservoir, and a waxy coating on the leaves themselves.

BELOW AND RIGHT *Some of the many different vein patterns found in simple and compound leaves:*

SIMPLE LEAVES

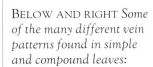

Pinnate venation

Palmate venation

Parallel venation

COMPOUND LEAVES

Pinnately compound

Bipinnately compound

Palmately compound

BELOW AND RIGHT *Some of the many different leaf forms and leaf margin shapes to be found:*

MARGINS

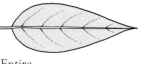

Entire

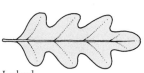

Lobed

Double serrate

SHAPES

Linear

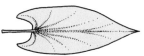

Sagittate

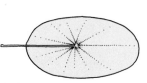

Peltate

PLANTS WITH SILVER-GREY FOLIAGE
Anthemis
Artemisia 'Powis Castle'
Ballota
Convolvulus cneorum
Cynara cardunculus
Cytisus × battandieri
Echinops
Eryngium giganteum
Lavandula
Lychnis coronaria
Melianthus major
Nepeta
Onopordum acanthium
Phlomis fruticosa
Santolina
Senecio 'Sunshine'
Stachys lanata
S. officinalis

LEAF ADAPTATIONS

One of the ways that gardeners can work out whether or not they are choosing the right site for a plant is by looking at its leaf formation.

Many plants that come from hotter parts of the world have greyish leaves, because the grey colouring helps to reflect the light and prevents the leaves from becoming too hot, which in turn helps to reduce water loss. Hairy, felted leaves also help to reduce water loss from the plant.

In other plants, leaves have adapted to reduce water loss by becoming fine and needle-like. This is particularly true of plants such as conifers from frozen parts of the world, where wind dries the moisture on the leaves. And as there is no water in the ground, because it is frozen, it is important that the leaves do not transpire too much water.

Plants that thrive in shade tend to have specially constructed leaves, to gather as much light as they can. Ivy leaves are arranged like tiles on a roof, held flat to the light, to obtain as much of it as possible.

Other woodland plants have adapted by having larger leaves and, as a result, many of the really handsome foliage plants are ideal for growing in shady places. The skunk cabbage (*Lysichiton americanus*), native to Alaska, likes semi-shaded damp conditions. Plantain lilies (*Hosta* sp.), from China and Japan, have large ribbed leaves to gather both light and moisture. In other plants, such as the giant Himalayan lily (*Cardocrinum giganteum*) leaves are arranged spirally around the plant to ensure maximum exposure to the light.

QUIRKS OF NATURE

Occasionally nature produces an oddity, a leaf without colouring, rather like an albino in the animal kingdom. Clearly a leaf that has no green colouring has no chlorophyll and therefore cannot absorb sunlight. Although you see plenty of variegated foliage plants introduced by man, they are rare in nature, simply because variegated leaves do not function as efficiently as plain green ones.

However, mankind – always keen to think that it is possible to improve on nature – has spotted these oddly coloured leaves or shoots, and taken cuttings from them (see page 80). But because the change from green to variegated is simply a mutation, the leaf can change back (revert) at any time. The growth rate on the green parts of the plant outstrips that on the variegated parts, since the latter do not photosynthesize as well, owing to their lack of pigmentation.

One of the families of plants in which variegation has been selected and bred from, to an extraordinary degree, is the pelargonium family (*Pelargonium* sp.), many species of which are grown as much for their leaf patterning as for their flowers. Another equally spectacular group of variegated foliage plants is the *Coleus* genus (now *Solenostemon*) from Java, with their wonderfully coloured, nettle-shaped leaves.

PLANTS WITH VARIEGATED LEAVES

Trees
Acer negundo
 'Flamingo'
Crataegus monogyna
 'Variegata'
Fagus sylvatica
 'Variegata'
Ligustrum
 lucidum 'Tricolor'
Platanus × hispanica
 'Suttneri'
Populus × candicans
 'Aurora'

Shrubs
Aucuba japonica
 'Crotonifolia'

Buddleia davidii
 'Harlequin'
Elaeagnus × ebbingei
 'Gilt Edge'
Hebe 'Purple Tips'
Ilex aquifolium 'Silver
 Queen'
Sambucus nigra
 'Pulverulenta'

Climbers
Actinidia kolomikta
Ampelopsis
 brevipedunculata
 'Elegans'
Hedera colchica 'Dentata
 Variegata'

Jasminum officinale
 'Aureum'
Lonicera japonica
 'Auroereticulata'
Trachelospermum
 jasminoides 'Variegata'

Conifers
Calocedrus decurrens
 'Aureovariegata'
Chamaecyparis
 lawsoniana 'White
 Spot'
C. pisifera 'Nana
 Variegata'
Juniperus chinensis
 'Variegata'

× Cupressocyparis
 leylandii 'Harlequin'
Thuja plicata 'Zebrina'

Herbaceous perennials
Brunnera macrophylla
 'Dawson's White'
Iris foetidissima
 'Variegata'
Lamiastrum galeobdolon
 'Variegatum'
Polygonatum falcatum
 'Variegatum'
Sedum alboroseum
 'Mediovariegatum'
Tolmiea menziesii 'Taff's
 Gold'

GUNNERA MANICATA

This herbaceous perennial has the largest leaves of any plant in cultivation. When you think that the number of pores on a square centimetre of an apple leaf is roughly 40,000, and that a gunnera leaf may have a span of more than 2m (6½ ft), you can only guess at the quantities of pores on each leaf and at its transpiration rate. The reason the leaves are so large is that the gunnera grows in the tropical rain forests of Brazil, and it needs to take advantage of the low light levels on the forest floor. The speed with which the plant leaps into life in spring is literally breathtaking, as it grows from almost nothing in winter to a height and spread of about 2.4 × 3.6 m (8 × 12ft) by early summer.

Although slightly tender, the gunnera can be grown in temperate climates, but it needs plenty of moisture in the soil, copious watering during the summer and a good supply of nutrients to support the massive leaf canopy. In winter, you should protect the coconut-sized crowns from frost by wrapping the leaves over them.

LEFT *Although a native of South America, gunnera will grow in temperate climates if it is given some protection for its crowns during the winter.*

STRATEGIES FOR SURVIVAL

In order to deter potential enemies, plants have adopted various strategies. Tender new leaves are particularly vulnerable to attack.

Among the arsenal of weapons that plants have at their disposal are thorns, spines and prickles, which are particularly effective at preventing the plant from being consumed by animals. Some plants, such as hawthorn (*Crataegus* sp.) and blackthorn (*Prunus spinoso*), have short, very sharp thorns growing out from the stem. Other plants, such as many of the cacti, have fierce spines, which are modified leaves. Still others have hooked prickles on stems, leaves or even on fruit. In addition to deterring small animals, these hooked prickles help the plant to support itself. In most cases the prickles are recurved – downward-pointing – which increases their chance of hooking themselves

LEFT *The common stinging nettle* (Urtica dioica) *protects itself from predators by the hairs that cover its stem, which create a painful rash on the skin of anyone who touches them. Despite this defence mechanism, nettles are invaluable plants for the wild garden, as they provide an important source of food for butterflies. For humans, the young leaves make delicious soup, or can be boiled and eaten, rather like spinach.*

into a support. Hairs are also a form of defence – the small hairs on leaves make them difficult for caterpillars to chew, while the hairs on the stems of the common stinging nettle (*Urtica dioica*) can penetrate the skin and inject a chemical that causes a painful rash.

A different form of chemical protection is provided by tannins, which some plants produce and which are found in leaves, unripe fruit, bark and roots. The presence of tannin makes the plant more resistant to insects and herbivorous animals, which dislike the astringent taste as much as humans do.

You can detect the presence of tannins, if you bite into an unripe apple – it tastes extremely sour. As the fruit matures, these tannins break down and are replaced by increasing quantities of sugar, leading to the sweetness associated with ripe fruit. One of the plants whose tannin content is familiar to us is the grape vine (*Vitis* sp.) and various vines have different degrees of tannin present, depending on the type of grape and the ripeness when harvested. The astringency of the tannin content lends character to the wine.

Other bitter-tasting chemicals, known as alkaloids, are present in some plants and have been found to have medicinal properties, if used in small quantities, but poisonous ones in larger quantities. Many of the mood-changing hallucinogenic drugs – including 'magic mushrooms', nicotine, cocaine and morphine – are based on alkaloids. In his use of these man has occasionally perverted the purpose of nature!

Some plants have very toxic chemicals in certain parts only. Rhubarb stems, for example, are good to eat, but the leaves can kill you. The fruit of the tomato plant is delicious, but its roots and shoots, again, can prove fatal, if eaten. In other plants, it is the fruit or seeds that must be avoided at all costs. Everyone knows that the fruit of deadly nightshade (*Solanum* sp., a member of the potato family) is poisonous, and that *Laburnum* seeds are notoriously dangerous for children, as are those of the castor bean (*Ricinus communis*).

A less virulent form of protection is camouflage. The most extreme form is that of the plants called 'living stones' (*Lithops* sp.), which come from the deserts of South Africa, and which so closely resemble stones that almost any animal is fooled by them.

Some genera, such as *Pieris* and *Photinia*, have red pigment in their leaves, possibly to convince insects that the leaves will taste horrible, or in the hope that insects will be confused by the brilliant coloration.

SOME POISONOUS HOUSE AND GARDEN PLANTS

PLANT	TOXIC PART	PLANT	TOXIC PART
Anemone (*Anemone tuberosum*)	all parts	Mistletoe (*Viscum* sp.)	berries
Apricot (*Prunus armeniacea*)	seeds, leaves	Monkshood (*Aconitum* sp.)	roots, seeds
Asparagus (*Asparagus officinalis*)	berries	Morning-glory (*lpomoea tricolor*)	seeds
Azalea (*Rhododendron* sp.)	all parts	Mountain laurel (*Kalmia latifolia*)	entire plant
Buttercup (*Ranunculus* sp.)	all parts	Oleander (*Nerium oleander*)	entire plant, esp. leaves
Caladium (*Caladium bicolor*)	leaves, tubers		
Croton (*Croton* sp.)	seeds	Peach (*Prunus persica*)	leaves, seeds
Crown-of-thorns (*Euphorbia milii*)	all parts	Poinsettia (*Euphorbia pulcherrima*)	leaves, stems, milky sap
Datura (*Datura* sp.)	seeds, leaves		
Eggplant (*Solanum melongena*)	leaves, stems	Potato (*Solanum tuberosum*)	leaves, stems, green tubers, sprouts
Foxglove (*Digitalis* sp.)	all parts		
Gloriosa lily (*Gloriosa* sp.)	tubers		
Holly (*Ilex* sp.)	berries	Privet (*Ligustrum japonicum*)	leaves, berries
Hydrangea (*Hydrangea* sp.)	all parts	Rhododendron (*Rhododendron* sp.)	all parts
Iris (*Iris* sp.)	leaves, rhizomes	Rhubarb (*Rheum* sp.)	leaf blades
Ivy (*Hedera helix*)	berries, leaves	Sweet pea (*Lathyrus* sp.)	seeds
Lantana (*Lantana* sp.)	berries	Tomato (*Lycopersicon esculenta*)	leaves, stems
Lily-of-the-valley (*Convallaria majalis*)	all parts	Virginia creeper (*Parthenocissus quinquefolia*)	berries
Lobelia (*Lobelia cardinalis*)	all parts	Wisteria (*Wisteria* sp.)	pods, seeds
Lupin (*Lupinus* sp.)	all parts	Yew (*Taxus baccata*)	all parts

GROWING FROM SEED

The production of seed is a fascinating process, which starts with pollination, in which the transference of pollen from one flower to another makes fertilization possible.

Not all flowers have the same pollination potential, but the majority of cultivated plants have bisexual flowers that contain both male and female parts, and so self-pollination can easily occur. Such a plant is therefore self-fertile, as is the whole of the rose family. The 'Victoria' plum is also self-fertile and is a member of the same family.

Some plants have unisexual flowers, in which the male and female parts are carried in separate flowers, although there are plants, such as the ornamental shrub *Akebia*, which bear both types of flower. If plants have male or female flowers only, it is important to know this, if you are growing plants for their decorative fruit. For instance, the sea-buckthorn (*Hippophae rhamnoides*) needs a mate in order for its brilliant orange berries to be produced, so, unless a neighbour has a specimen, you will need both male and female plants, although obviously only the female forms bear fruit.

To complicate the story still further, some species can have both unisexual and bisexual flowers on the same plant, or on different plants. These are called polygamous, examples being the climbing bittersweet (*Celastrus orbiculatus*), with its spectacular red and yellow

LEFT *Butterflies, like this Painted Lady* (Vanessa cardui) *feeding on Allium* neapolitanum, *and bees, as well as other insects, play a vital part in the pollination process.*

RIGHT *This cross-section of a cherry flower shows the various parts of the plant that perform a function in fertilization, as the pollen is transferred from the anthers to the stigma.*

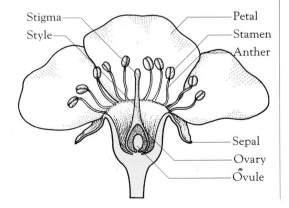

Stigma
Style
Petal
Stamen
Anther
Sepal
Ovary
Ovule

fruits, and the viburnum (*Viburnum davidii*), whose brilliantly blue berries last throughout the winter.

As far as pollination is concerned, cross-pollination is preferable to prevent inbreeding and weakening of the race. In this context, cross-pollination refers to pollination between two flowers from different plants. But in botanical terms, cross-pollination means the movement of pollen from one flower to another on the same plant, as well as from a flower on a different plant.

FERTILIZATION

The fact that pollination has taken place does not necessarily mean that fertilization automatically occurs. The stigma of the flower may have received pollen, but without suitable conditions the pollen grains will not develop and will die quite quickly. The pollen has to be ripe and the stigma must be receptive. And if the stigma is being fertilized by pollen from anthers in the same flower, it should not be out of reach of the anthers. Cold or dry atmospheric conditions inhibit germination of the pollen, and if the pollen reaches a flower of a different genus altogether, it will not develop.

Some plants are completely self-incompatible; for instance, there are so many fruiting cherry cultivars of this type that tables have had to be drawn up showing groups of cherries, with each group consisting of pollinators for another group.

Pollen grains need a growing medium in which to develop, and this is the sugary solution produced either by the stigma responding to the presence of the pollen grain, or by the cells of the style. The pollen then produces a short tube that grows down the style to the ovary, which it enters, and from this fusion the embryo is created and thus the seed is formed, from which a new plant will grow.

Similarly, self-pollination in botanical terms means that a flower is pollinated by the pollen it produces itself whereas, for breeding purposes, self-pollination is said to occur between any flowers of the same plant. Therefore, if you want to produce plants that are different from their parents, you must cross-pollinate between flowers of two different plants, though it does not actually matter whether the plants are bisexual or unisexual.

DISPERSAL OF POLLEN

Pollen is spread by a variety of agents, in the same way that seeds are, and these agents include water (rarely), wind and insects. Flowers that rely on wind for their pollination produce vast quantities of pollen, from stamens that stand well clear of the petals or bracts. It is these flowers and their masses of pollen that are largely responsible for the onset of hay-fever in humans.

BELOW *The reproductive process: the pollen grains land on the stigma of the flower, and when they have germinated they move down through the style. The pollen then enters the ovule to fertilize the egg inside.*

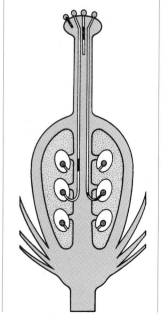

FLOWERS AND THEIR POLLINATING INSECTS

No flowers are visited solely by the insects specified; these are simply the principal ones, and many other types of insect will be involved from time to time.

Arum	flies
Borage	honey-bees
Buddleia	butterflies
Daffodil	bumble-bees
Daisy	flies
Figwort	wasps
Foxglove	bumble-/honey-bees
Honeysuckle	privet hawk moths
Pheasant's-eye narcissus	moths
Primrose	honey-bees
Rose	beetles
Sweet pea	bumble-bees
Sunflower	beetles
Thyme	honey-bees
Yucca	moths

ABOVE *A bumble-bee diligently at work collecting pollen from a sunflower.*

But it is insects that play the greatest part in pollination, although this is quite fortuitous: they visit many flowers for many different reasons, but not specifically to distribute pollen. Certainly the presence of pollen is one reason, as it is a food for many of them; so too is nectar, and the insect may be of the kind that lays eggs within the flower. In any of these processes, pollen will brush off on to the insect's body, and will then either fall or be knocked off on to the female parts of the next flower that it visits.

Honey-bees and butterflies are the most well-known pollinating insects, but wasps, beetles, flies and moths all visit flowers and carry on the good work.

The average garden will be alive with a variety of flower-visiting insects, and the deliberate cultivation of butterfly and bee flowers in particular will greatly add to its attractions, and will help in the setting of fruit as well as the production of seed and ornamental seed heads. It is also well worth bearing in mind that many weeds – often native wild species – will attract pollinating insects to what can be highly ornamental flowers.

Butterfly plants include the following: Michaelmas daisy, buddleia, *Sedum spectabile*, lavender, scabious, stock, catmint, hyssop, honesty, golden rod, petunia, mignonette, pink, honeysuckle and sea thrift. Bee plants include: lupin, bluebell, foxglove, lungwort, monkshood, chives, godetia, cotoneaster, nasturtium, sea lavender, alyssum, clarkia and globe thistle.

THE SEED

One of the most enjoyable activities in gardening is to produce new plants from seed. Out of a small – sometimes minuscule – seed develops a complex and beautiful plant.

So what is a seed, and how does it start to grow? The seed contains an embryo plant; and there will also be nutrients, either within the embryo or within a structure – the endosperm – which can be used by the developing seedling after germination. Within that embryo is the blueprint for the adult plant, anything from a sweet pea to an oak tree – all the instructions for the varied shapes and colours are found within the cells of the embryo, and there is nothing more magical than watching the development from seed that you have sown yourself. As the first tiny signs of the leaf appear above the soil, from an apparently inert piece of matter, a miracle really does seem to be taking place.

In order that plants may increase, the seeds they produce need to be small, relatively speaking, and need to keep well over a long period. Their moisture content is low and their metabolism ticks over extremely slowly. Even at this early stage, though, the embryo consists of a root tip (radicle) attached to a stem-like object (hypocotyl), at the top end of which, furthest from the root tip, are the cotyledons, commonly and erroneously known as the seed leaves. The whole is enclosed in, and covered by, the seed coat (testa). Flowering plant families are divided into two major groups: the dicotyledons, which have two cotyledons to each seed, and the monocotyledons, which have only one, and of which grasses, lilies and sedges are examples.

Seeds vary enormously in size, from the dust-like particles of begonias to the large stone of avocado pears, and the even larger 'nut' of the coconut palm. However, there are many which, although small, are of manageable size for the gardener – for instance, those of tomatoes, Brussels sprouts, wallflower and marigold. Such seeds are easily sown, but the tiny ones need special techniques (see page 111).

On the whole, the basic seed shape is round or oval, but often with attachments, depending on its method of dispersal. Sometimes seeds are 'pelleted' by seed companies to make sowing easier; and the coating may also contain fungicide and nutrients, to ensure that the seedling has defences as well as extra food to help it to establish itself.

SEED DISPERSAL

There is a variety of ways in which seeds ensure that they have the opportunity to spread and germinate at some distance from their parent, and thus ensure that the species survives and increases.

BELOW *The features of a seed: the external and internal features, showing the thick seed coat, or testa, on the outside (top) and the internal embryo (below), with its future root (radicle), shoot (plumule) and leaf (cotyledon) in place.*

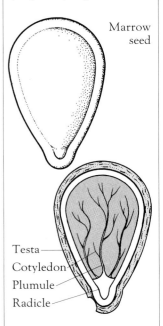

Marrow seed

Testa
Cotyledon
Plumule
Radicle

Broad bean seed

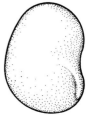

THE SQUIRTING CUCUMBER

The squirting cucumber, *Ecballium elaterium*, is a common weed found in subtropical Mediterranean regions, forming a roughly hairy, trailing plant with a spread of about 60cm (2ft). It is a member of the same family as marrows and cucumbers, the *Cucurbitaceae* family, with similarly shaped leaves, small yellow flowers and hairy fruit only about 5–7.5cm (2–3in) long. When ripe, they need only to be touched to explode violently, enough to make an unwary walker jump, and the seed is spat out in a kind of jelly. The juice is acrid and the plant itself poisonous.

RIGHT *The swollen fruit of the squirting cucumber, ready to burst at the slightest touch. The seed can be expelled a distance of up to 2.5m (8ft).*

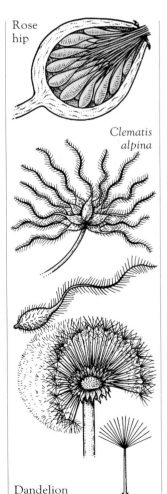

Rose hip

Clematis alpina

Dandelion

Wind is one of the most obvious methods of dispersal, and there are garden plants with some delightful adaptations to their seeds for this purpose. *Clematis alpina*, for example, has blue flowers that develop what are technically fruit, each containing a seed, and each with a long silky-hairy style attached. Arranged in a whorl around the centre of the flower, they curve backwards towards the stalk and persist for many weeks, looking like old-man's-beard, but silky and gleaming rather than grey and fluffy.

The 'clock' of the dandelion (*Taraxacum officinale*) is one of the best-known examples of wind pollination, each seed having its own parachute of hairs. And the down of thistles (*Cirsium* sp.) is notorious for its invading abilities.

Some seeds have adapted differently, and the fruits containing them have developed 'wings', like those of the sycamore (*Acer pseudoplatanus*). Gladiolus seeds are also, surprisingly, winged, as are the seeds of

SEED DISPERSAL
Plants have evolved different ways of dispersing their seed so that it gains the optimum chance of survival. In the hips of roses, the fleshy fruit swells and bursts, or is eaten by birds, and the seed is dispersed as a result; clematis and dandelions have light parachutes of hairs attached to each seed or seed stalk, enabling them to be carried a long distance by the wind; geranium seeds are dispersed by an explosive opening mechanism.

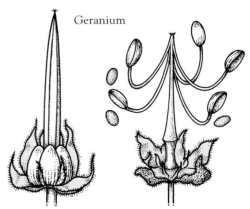

Geranium

conifer, lime (*Tilia cordata*) and hornbeam (*Carpinus betulus*). Such seeds are likely to germinate in unexpected places, and if you find sycamore seedlings in a garden without a sycamore tree in sight, look at the neighbours' gardens or any nearby woodland. This characteristic also shows the desirability of removing flowers from weeds before they mature to seedling stage; dandelion seed looks pretty, but a dandelion's tap root goes down deep into the ground.

All sorts of animals, including humans, become unwitting carriers of seeds. Quite often seed is moved about by ants, especially in dry summers, which favour their nest-building activities. The seedlings of both weeds and cultivated plants often come up unexpectedly in crevices in paving, as a result.

Many fruit seeds, with their fleshy, succulent covering, are dispersed by animals. Sometimes the seed is easy to get at for the gardener, as with the pips of oranges or apples, and the process is enjoyable too! Slugs, beetles and birds all help in their diffusion as they gnaw or peck at the fruit.

Some seeds have adapted to animal dispersal by developing hooks, which readily become attached to fur or hair as the animals brush past them. The 'sticky' round balls of cleavers (*Galium aparine*) easily hook on to clothing, and so do the hooks of burdock (*Arctium* sp.) and geum (*Geum* sp.).

Other seeds, like hazelnuts, chestnuts, the 'mast' of beech and acorns, are eaten by animals, not necessarily immediately, but sometimes from stores previously collected. Squirrels are a case in point and occasionally other rodents will do the same. Having buried the seeds, they may then forget them, so that the following spring the nut or acorn may germinate well away from its parent tree.

Birds play their part by eating seeds of many kinds, whether exposed and obvious, as in the case of yew (*Taxus* sp.), or contained within a fleshy fruit. Hawthorn, spindleberry and blackberry are all popular in autumn, when the birds are stocking up for the winter. Interestingly, some seeds germinate better once they have been digested by the bird and have passed through it. And by the time this happens, the bird may have travelled a considerable distance, 80 kms (50 miles) or more.

Another method of dispersal, always intriguing when seen as it actually happens, is the explosive mechanism. Hairy bittercress (*Cardamine hirsuta*) is a small and, unfortunately, common annual weed, which the unwary gardener has merely to touch for its seed pods to explode with some force, scattering its seeds as much as 60cm (2ft) away. Shepherd's-purse (*Capsella bursa-pastoris*) is another weed to beware of in this respect, but broom, lupins and gorse – the ejected seeds of which may be caught by the wind and spread even further – are garden plants whose seedlings can be worth nurturing.

VIABILITY OF VEGETABLE SEEDS

NAME	NO. OF YEARS
Beetroot	4
Broad bean	2
Broccoli	3
Brussels sprouts	3
Cabbage	3
Carrot	4
Cauliflower	3
Celeriac	6
Celery	6
Cucumber	7
French bean	2
Kale	3
Leek	4
Lettuce	4
Marrow	7
Mustard/cress	3
Onion	4
Parsley	2
Parsnip	1
Pea	2
Radish	4
Runner bean	2
Salsify	2
Scorzonera	1
Spinach	2
Spinach beet (perpetual spinach)	4
Swede	2
Tomato	5
Turnip	2

Some vegetables will continue to be viable after these periods, but the percentage viability will drop dramatically.

GERMINATION

Although a seed may appear to be lifeless, it is essential to remember that it is, usually, very much alive, with the potential for changing from its inert state to an actively growing one. Seeds can remain viable like this for many years – dock seed, for example, can be viable for 50 years or more, and the Japanese have recently reported a case of seed thousands of years old germinating normally.

In general, however, a few years is the maximum, with some seeds losing their viability quite quickly after ripening and being shed, so that it always pays to sow seed soon after it is ripe. At this stage it has usually changed colour, often becoming a shade of brown, or black. It will be loosely attached to the plant, if it has not already dropped or been dispersed, and it may already be germinating on the plant.

In order for germination to take place, moisture is needed. When the seed is shed, it will already have a certain percentage of moisture present, which enables it to survive until the conditions are right for germination. Moisture from soil or compost is absorbed, as a result of which the cotyledons swell and the seed coat eventually splits.

Until this occurs, the seed does not need oxygen and the first stages of germination take place anaerobically (without oxygen). But once the seed coat has split, oxygen is essential so that respiration can be carried on. One of the reasons for proper seedbed preparation is to ensure that the soil structure is loose enough to allow for good aeration – a compacted soil will be starved of oxygen. A well-prepared seedbed will be moisture-retentive without being waterlogged, providing the developing seedlings with reserves of water on which to call as they grow.

The temperature of the growing medium is another crucial factor. Too low, and germination will not take place; but too high a temperature for the particular seed species in question will, surprisingly, have the same effect.

In cool-temperate climates the range of temperature is usually between 4 and 21°C (40 and 70°F), with hardy seeds germinating well in a range of 10–18°C (50–65°F). Half-hardy seeds germinate better at between 16 and 21°C (60 and 70°F). In general, the higher the temperature that the plant would naturally grow in, the higher the temperature required for germination – about 5°C (10°F) above normal growing conditions for the adult plant.

Another important factor in germination is the presence or absence of light. Darkness is advisable if temperatures are low, but some seeds will not germinate unless they are exposed to light, and are either sown on the surface or are only lightly covered with compost. In the case of

ORANGE PIPS AND THEIR SEEDLINGS

Oranges can easily be grown from pips, and indeed when some oranges are opened up, the pips will already be germinating inside. But in general they need to be sown, giving them warmth of about 27°C (80°F) and placing them about 1.5cm (½in) deep in seed compost. They will germinate at slightly lower temperatures, but rather more slowly. You will find that one orange pip produces several seedlings. This is because orange pips are polyembryonic (that is, they contain several embryos). One of the seedlings will be hybrid, resulting from normal male/female fertilization, and it will therefore be unlike the parent; the other seedlings will be identical to it, and are called nucellar embryos. In commercial practice they are used as stocks for grafting. Both kinds usually take several years to fruit.

bigger seeds, such as peas or beans, sowing below the surface helps to anchor them and ensures that the whole of the seed coat absorbs the moisture. However, many seeds are indifferent to the presence or absence of light and will germinate under both conditions. Where light is definitely required, red light has the most influence, but infra-red light, on the other hand, can inhibit germination.

Once the seed has absorbed water, the cotyledons have started to swell and the seed coat has split, the root tip will be the first part of the seedling to emerge. This is followed by elongation of the stem-like hypocotyl, and the stem tip (plumule) then expands from between the cotyledons and, as it lengthens, the first true leaf opens out from it.

At the same time, the root tip sprouts secondary roots, and it is at this stage in the plant's existence that it has the greatest need for the mineral nutrient phosphorus. Otherwise the developing seedling will exist on the food reserves within the seed, either inside the embryo itself or in the tissue that surrounds it. These reserves consist of starch, liquid fat, mineral nutrients, vitamins and hormones. Sometimes the main reserves are in the cotyledons, which are then thick, as in broad bean seeds, and consist mostly of protein and starch.

There are two types of germination: epigeal, and hypogeal. In the former case, the cotyledons burst out of the seed coat and grow above the soil to form the so-called seed leaves, which then start their photosynthetic process. Lupin (*Lupinus* sp.) seeds are an example of epigeal germination, but the broad bean is hypogeal – its cotyledons never actually appear above the soil or compost. Peas and runner beans are similar and, if you sow peas in pots, you will see that the emerging stem is pointed, and then almost at once develops the three-parted true leaves. There is no interim seed leaf stage, and the seed relies on its reserves to keep it going for longer than the epigeal type.

Depth of sowing is important; too deeply sown (often the case with vegetable seeds), and the embryonic shoots cannot struggle up to the shallower level to obtain the oxygen that they need. This problem can be further compounded by lack of light, bearing in mind that in

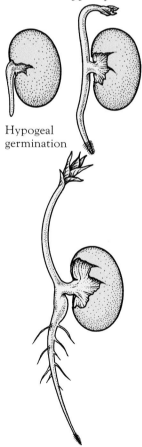

BELOW AND RIGHT In broad beans the stem emerges first, curled up to protect it as it passes through the soil. This is called hypogeal germination. Marrows develop by epigeal germination, in which the seed leaves appear first.

Hypogeal germination

Epigeal germination

nature seeds are shed on to the soil surface and germinate without ever being covered.

But if seeds are not covered, when being sown, they may blow away or be eaten by birds. The answer is to ensure that they are anchored and that there is enough of a blanket to maintain a moisture supply; given these requirements, it is better to err on the side of a light covering rather than a heavy one.

While seeds come packed with a food supply, this will quickly be used up. Photosynthesis will partly fill the resulting gap with starches and carbon dioxide, but mineral nutrients, such as nitrogen and phosphorus, will be required as the root tip extends and secondary roots develop. Annual plants absorb most of their entire life's need for phosphorus from the soil during the first few days after germination, and for any young plant this mineral must be available. Nitrogen will be also needed for the stem, leaf and shoot growth of all plants, and a variety of other minerals will contribute to various aspects of a plant's growth and health.

Generally there will be sufficient minerals present in most open-ground soils for many weeks of growth, but in seed-composts seedlings will need to be transplanted, as soon as they are large enough to handle, to a food-containing potting compost.

CAUSES OF NON-GERMINATION

It is disappointing in the extreme when your long-awaited seedlings fail to emerge.

Lack of moisture is often the cause of failure to germinate. Sowing in dry soil or compost, or during a drought, is a waste of time. And the right kind of light – or not, as the case may be – and a suitable temperature for the species concerned are also vital; and, once germination has started, oxygen and nutrients must be available. A lack of any of these will, at the very least, delay germination; or germination may start but the new growth may wither; or there may not be any germination at all.

Another reason may be that the succulent young shoots have been devoured by slugs, soil-living caterpillars, seed-beetles or similar underground plant pests. A further possibility is that the seed, especially the fleshy kinds like peas and beans, has rotted in a cold, wet soil or compost before or after germination, due to infection by fungal diseases in the soil.

RIGHT *Beech seedlings emerging after germination: the failure rate of many seeds to germinate in nature is high.*

DORMANCY

It is quite possible to provide all the seed's requirements in the right quantities and still not catalyse it into life. Many seeds, especially those of weeds (wild flowers), shrubs and trees become dormant when shed, and need special treatment to trigger the growth process. In effect the seed waits until the conditions in its natural habitat are right for germination – some seeds need to go through specific climatic changes before sprouting.

If a seed does not germinate within two weeks (three at the outside) – given that it is fresh, has been stored in suitable conditions and obtained from a reliable source – it may have become dormant. Sometimes this is a mechanical dormancy, in that the seed has a hard coat impermeable to water except after a long period.

Sweet peas (*Lathyrus odoratus*), for instance, germinate very much more quickly if the outside of the seed is chipped with a sharp knife or razor blade, making a tiny cut just through the seed coat. For safety's sake, so that the embryo inside is not injured, make the cut away from any obvious lines or scars, where the seed was attached to the parent. Alternatively, try sand-papering or filing the seed coat to reduce its thickness, rather than actually breaking it.

Soaking in hot water is another method, especially useful for tropical plants such as the seed of the bird-of-paradise plant (*Strelitzia reginae*) or the canna lily (*Canna* sp.). Use only a little water, which has just boiled, and leave the seed to soak for at least 24 hours.

STRATIFICATION

A more sophisticated way of softening a hard seed coat is called stratification. It is especially useful for rose hips, holly berries and the stones

BELOW *Stratification: place the seeds in a pot filled with a mixture of sand and soil, covered with perforated zinc sheet, and bury in the ground. Leave over the winter, or longer, until germination takes place. Inspect periodically to see if this has occurred.*

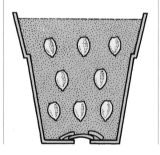

GROWING PARSLEY FROM SEED

Parsley has a bad reputation for non-germination, or very slow germination, taking four or five weeks when sown outdoors. It is commonly sown in March or April and may not appear until mid-April or May, depending on the time of sowing. Part of the problem is undoubtedly that slugs and snails eat the seedlings immediately they appear, and if you do not examine the seedbed daily, you will miss what brief life the seedlings have.

But although parsley is regarded as a hardy plant, its seed does not like cold soil, which makes sense when you remember that the seed is naturally produced and shed in June–July. Seed deliberately sown in early midsummer will germinate within days and provide good leaf for the winter.

To hasten germination in the spring, cover the soil outdoors two or three weeks in advance of sowing – but not when there is already frost in the ground! Choose a day for covering when the sun is warming the soil. Sow the seed in peat that has just been watered with hot water, and protect the sowing until germination occurs.

SAVING HOME-GROWN SEED

There is no reason why you should not use seed produced by your own garden plants, and there are several advantages of doing so. First, it is cheap. Second, you can ensure that the seed has been grown without the use of pesticides or artificial fertilizers. Third, over the years you can select strong or heavy-bearing strains of crops, or new or particularly colourful ornamentals. Finally, you can often continue to grow old fruit and vegetable varieties from your own seed, which you cannot buy from seedsmen, since there are certain varieties that it is now illegal to sell under EC law. (They are therefore no longer listed by seedsmen, although they should still be available from seed banks.)

When choosing suitable plants, use the strongest of a group. The plants should be healthy and free from disease, particularly virus, which is not curable, and they should be as representative of the type as possible. For this to occur it is a good idea – if flower or flowers are self-fertile, or if there are different varieties of the same species in the garden – to bag them with gauze or brown paper. However, if you are interested in the possibility of growing something different there is no need to prevent cross-pollination from taking place, and in any case seed does not breed 100 per cent true.

Collect the seed on a dry day – damp seed will not keep – from plants whose seed pods have ceased to change colour and are about to split open; many will be dry and crackly. Initially collect the seed pods in paper bags with a good length of stem attached to each, and label each bag clearly, at the time of collection. It is all too easy to collect first and label later,

only to discover that you cannot then remember which seeds have which coloured flowers, from which varieties.

To dry the seed, hang up the seed pods, head-downwards, or spread them out on trays lined with paper, to finish ripening and drying in a warm, sunny place, free from draught or wind. This will take only a few days in most cases. Many seeds will loosen and shake free of their pods or cases naturally; those that remain should be cleaned by being shaken or gently rubbed through a sieve, rubbed between the fingers, or they can be rolled with a bottle or rolling pin. If the seed is dust-like, you may have to accept that some chaff remains, in order not to lose too much of the seed.

Finally, put the cleaned seed into manilla envelopes or other suitable paper (not plastic) packets, label and place in an airtight container in the dark, to which you have added silica gel, or a few grains of rice or anhydrous calcium chloride, to absorb any moisture. Seal the container, then keep it at a constant cool temperature of about 10°C (50°F) until the seed is required.

VEGETABLE SEEDS WORTH SAVING

Beans	Parsnip
Beetroot	Pea
Carrot	Perpetual spinach
Cucumber	Salsify
Leek	Scorzonera
Lettuce	Spinach (summer and winter)
Marrow	Swiss chard
Onion	Tomato

of fruit such as peaches or plums. The method consists of placing the berries or stones in layers in a mixture of moist coarse sand, or moist half-sand and half-peat, or peat alternative, such as coir or vermiculite. Shallow pots (pans) or boxes can be used, half-filling them and then spacing the fruit or stones out evenly on the surface, finally covering them to fill the container.

Put the pots or boxes outdoors plunged into soil or ashes, and cover with perforated zinc sheet for the winter to prevent mice from feeding on the contents. Germination may occur in spring, or not until 12–18 months later. Where berries are concerned, provided that the pulp has disintegrated, the seeds can be retrieved and sown, separately, otherwise they are likely to germinate in a tight cluster.

LEFT *The seed of the field poppy* (Papaver rhoeas) *can stay dormant for decades – seed over 60 years old has been known to germinate; many seeds need very specific conditions before they will break dormancy.*

CHILLING

The seeds of many hardy plants will not germinate unless they have a period of really cold temperatures after they have been shed, not necessarily to break dormancy, but to allow the embryo time to mature. Stratification can be used for such seeds, as outdoor temperatures in cool-temperate climates nearly always drop below freezing in winter. Moreover, the alternation that frequently occurs between cold and relatively warm periods from autumn to spring seems to be beneficial in breaking dormancy.

It is also possible to break dormancy in this way by putting the seed in a domestic refrigerator for about four weeks at a temperature of 3–5°C (38–43°F). The seed should be moist – it can be soaked in cold water for 24 hours first – and placed in vermiculite, peat, coir or sand in a pot or plastic bag. Keep an eye on the contents and examine them frequently as germination time approaches.

DOUBLE DORMANCY

Where there may be what is known as a double dormancy, of the shoot as well as the root, as with some lilies and ash (*Frexinus excelsior*), a warm period is needed first in order for the root tip to start into growth. This should last for about three months and be in the region of 21–30°C (70–85°F), roughly equivalent to a cool-temperate summer, followed by three months of cold, which ensures that the cotyledons and hypocotyl begin to develop and that germination starts in earnest.

SOWING SEED

For the sake of convenience the best time to sow the majority of seeds in cool-temperate climates is the spring, any time from early March to mid-May. Although some seeds, particularly herbs, germinate most satisfactorily if sown when fresh (that is, just after they have ripened and been shed), there are others that may have become dormant for some weeks or months, or that are indifferent to their state of maturity. Viability may drop quickly or slowly.

In general, the season when growth is starting – and when both soil and air temperature are rising, and day length is increasing – is the most suitable one for sowing both ornamentals and crops.

Autumn can also be a good time to sow outdoors. At the end of the summer there is a kind of secondary spring, when plants start to grow again. The old country saying about 40 days' drought following a dry St Swithun's Day on 15 July often actually holds good, in that the weather frequently breaks in the last week in August, with cloud and

RIGHT *Dandelion seeds disperse via the parachutes of hairs attached to each seed. Nature ensures that seeds disperse to increase their chances of survival. Gardeners increase these chances by providing optimum soil conditions: a fine tilth, adequate moisture and warmth.*

rain that lay the dust and revive the garden. The moist environment, together with the warmth of soil and air, provide ideal germinating conditions; most experienced gardeners will know that this is the time that weeds start to encroach again as well!

The weather is, in fact, one of the most crucial factors in the germination of seed sown in the open ground. If there has been too much rain, the soil will be too wet to transform it to the seedbed tilth required, and if some of the moisture is due to melted snow, the soil will be cold as well.

On the other hand, it is beneficial if the sowing time can be chosen when rain is forecast, so that you do not have to resort to hand watering, since the seed should never lack moisture in its early stages.

A cold soil will inhibit germination, even of hardy seeds, and if cold is combined with wet for long enough, the seed may rot or, if germination has started, the embryo shoots may be invaded by fungus disease or destroyed by frost. Covering the soil with plastic sheet, cloches, old carpet, even newspaper, some days in advance will help if early sowing is unavoidable, and keeping the seeds well protected by cloches is a further safeguard.

Much advice is given on the production of a seedbed and the state that the soil should be in to ensure good germination of seed. In the Victorian vegetable garden a great deal of time was spent on producing the ideal tilth, and this advice has been handed down to the present day almost as holy writ.

But the modern garden generally does not offer sufficient space for an entire seedbed, and the modern gardener frequently does not have the necessary time to devote to it. In any case, the crumb-like tilth so often advocated is not always needed, particularly for bigger seeds.

In nature, seeds fall on to a very mixed surface of rotting leaves and stems – there will be woody twigs in various stages of decay, fruit, petals, sometimes a bare soil surface or one with cracks in it, and so on. But this 'growing medium' results in very hit-and-miss germination. Many seeds do not sprout at all – probably one of the reasons why nature arranges for the production of so many seeds in the first place. The gardener wants 100 per cent germination, so it pays to work on the soil in advance. If you do so, the soil particles will cluster together in crumbs, to allow for the exchange of air and soil gases in the space between them, and will also permit surplus rain to drain through after thoroughly moistening them. An entirely smooth surface would puddle, and prevent air from penetrating beneath it; a lumpy surface – besides being unevenly wet and dry – would overwhelm most of the seeds, and some would be uncovered and exposed to birds and wind.

A good compromise, when time and space are short, is to restrict soil preparation just to those areas where the seed is to be sown. For vegetables, this will generally be along lines where the drills are to be drawn out, and for ornamentals in patches in beds and borders. Of course, if you are proposing to fill a bed with annuals, then the entire area will have to be prepared, so a seedbed will be the end product.

For the highest rate of germination and subsequent strong seedling growth, the soil should be in a crumb-like state. This can be produced by forking and knocking down the bigger clods, using a hand fork to break them down still further, and raking to a depth of 4cm (1½in). Crumbling between the fingers is the quickest way of producing the final tilth for small areas, or raking twice crosswise for larger ones.

It goes without saying that weeds should be scrupulously eradicated, roots and all, and stones, sticks and general rubbish consigned to the dustbin. Any slugs and snails found during the proceedings can be eliminated, too. A firm sowing area enables the seedling roots to anchor themselves securely, and this can be done by heel-to-toe treading between the stages of forking and hand-forking.

But be warned – none of this can be achieved unless the soil has the right moisture content. Too dry, and the clods will not break up; too wet and it will not be possible to produce a crumb structure, only a lumpy one. Keep an eye on the soil and seize the opportunity as soon as it responds to handling.

If you are having difficulty in coinciding with this ideal soil state, there are one or two ways of cheating. Draw the drills out slightly deeper than required, and line them with moist peat or coir, then cover the seeds with the same material. Alternatively, use seed compost – this is especially useful for patch sowing, as the whole surface can be taken off and replaced.

SOWING IN DRILLS

The standard technique for vegetables is to sow in drills, that is, tiny furrows drawn out in a straight line with the corner of a hoe or the prongs of a hand fork.

First mark the place for the drill with cord that has been stretched between two sticks. Then dribble seed continuously and thinly along

RIGHT Most seed is sown in drills – shallow furrows that are drawn in very finely raked soil.

Make the drill with a sharp instrument, such as the corner of a hoe, in a straight line that has been marked with string.

Sow the seed thinly along the base of the drill.

Cover the drill lightly with soil and smooth with the back of a rake. Water well using the fine rose on a watering can.

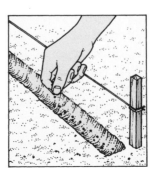

the base of the drill and cover it to the recommended depth only. Sowing seed too deep accounts for many of the failures to germinate.

STATION SOWING

This method is an alternative to continuous sowing. Several seeds are sown at evenly spaced intervals along the drill. It has the advantages of cutting down on thinning time and conserving seeds, and is often used for the larger seeds, such as parsnip. Beetroot seed is station-sown singly, as it is actually a fruit containing several seeds.

PATCH SOWING

Seed is sprinkled evenly over the surface of a given area and then covered. This method is used for ornamentals such as annuals, and for vegetables where young leaf is the prime requirement, or where vegetables are being grown to provide ornament as well.

NURSERY BEDS

An area that can be set aside outdoors as temporary accommodation for seeds and young plants is invaluable; it should be sunny, sheltered from the wind, and warm, but need not be too large. Winter-cropping vegetables that have to be sown in the spring can grow on here and so can biennial ornamentals, such as wallflowers (*Cheiranthus cheiri*) and sweet williams (*Dianthus barbatus*).

Shrub and tree seeds are other suitable candidates for nursery beds, as the seedlings need time to develop before being transplanted to their permanent sites.

SOWING IN CONTAINERS

Many plants germinate best if sown in pots or trays. Tender varieties can only be sown in containers if they are to flower in the same season, and often lack of space in today's gardens ensures that container sowing is the only option – there simply is no room for long-standing crops or nursery beds.

One enormous advantage of container-sowing is that the gardener has almost complete control over the conditions for germination and over the initial growth of the young plants. Water, food, light, warmth and oxygen can all be tailored to the seed's requirements. One hundred per cent successful germination is possible, given the sterile conditions of today's seed composts and the reliability of seed supplied by modern seedsmen.

The indoor seed-sowing season can start in February, with the help of heated propagators to maintain temperatures above 16°C (60°F). Such temperatures are needed for half-hardy varieties that are to flower or fruit in the coming summer, such as tomatoes, peppers,

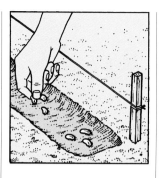

ABOVE *Station sowing: larger seeds can be sown at evenly spaced intervals along a drill, avoiding the need for thinning.*

pelargoniums or bedding begonias. March and April are the busiest months and, if your enthusiasm for growing plants got out of control when the seed catalogues came through the letterbox at Christmas, you will be hard put to find space for all the containers of seeds, seedlings and young plants growing on.

It is important to consider in advance how many containers you will want, and what kind you will be requiring. It pays to go round the garden centres in February to have a look at what is available, since the days when seeds were sown only in seed-trays are long gone. There is now a vast assortment, not the least of which are cellular plastic trays.

The individual cells of these trays vary in size from about 2.5–7.5cm (1–3in), so that they can be used for sowing seed and for pricking out seedlings. If you are hard-pressed for time and/or space, one or more seeds can be sown in a 4 or 5cm (1½ or 2in)-size cell and left to grow on until ready for planting outdoors or potting into a larger container (as would be necessary with tomatoes). Incidentally, this method is good for the seedling, which then suffers less disturbance and injury to its roots. The cell-trays last for several seasons, if handled with care. A pot or cell size of about 5cm (2in) and of a similar depth is one of the most useful for propagating. By the time seedling roots have filled it, the plant is of such a size that it is ready for planting and is unlikely to be attacked by slugs or snails – it is the small, juicy morsels, like newly germinated seedlings, that they prefer.

Other containers include seed-trays of 2.5 or 7.5cm (1 or 3in) depth – full size (32.5×15cm/13×6in), half-size or quarter – which are useful

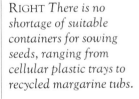

RIGHT *There is no shortage of suitable containers for sowing seeds, ranging from cellular plastic trays to recycled margarine tubs.*

for pricking out large quantities of seedlings, as well as for sowing seed. Pots can be of plastic or clay; peat and paper pots are particularly convenient, as they can be planted out complete. And there is a new development, Root-trainers, which are deep pots with internal grooves to guide the roots so that they grow straight downwards. These are good for deeply rooting plants, such as sweet peas.

There are several proprietary brands of seed compost available, devised to provide seeds with exactly the conditions they need for germination and subsequent growth. Most are peat-based, although peat-alternative composts are now appearing. John Innes seed-compost is soil-based, and can be made at home, provided the soil (loam) can be sterilized; otherwise it will contain weed seedlings, fungal diseases and insect pests.

Whatever temperature seeds are sown in, it should be constant during the day and night, although a small drop of about 2–3°C (5°F) from day to night is possible, and is sometimes necessary for some species. During the day 16–21°C (60–70°F) is a good average range; 21–27°C (70–80°F) is better for subtropical and tropical seeds. Electrically heated propagators with transparent, rigid, plastic covers are convenient to use, although airing cupboards can also be pressed into service temporarily.

Advice on sowing seed in the first part of this century included the need for covering the seed with newspaper and glass. This then changed to black plastic, to keep light out, as well as to retain moisture. Recent research has shown, however, that many varieties are unaffected by the presence or absence of light. Some seeds definitely need it, begonias and lettuce for instance; if in doubt, do not cover, but if germination seems to be protracted, then exclude the light – it may make a difference.

Ensure that your containers are clean and sterile before starting, as this reduces the risk of pest and disease problems after germination. As with outdoor sowing, it pays to make the seed compost level and evenly firm. Soil-based compost in a seed-tray should be firmed in with

BELOW Sowing seeds.

Fill the seed tray with sowing compost, or another suitable medium, make sure it is moist and then level and firm it.

Scatter the seed evenly over the surface of the compost or sow in lines, ensuring that they are as evenly spaced as possible.

If the seeds need to be covered with compost, sieve it over them. Finally, cover the seed tray with clingfilm or clear polythene and put in a light, but not sunny, place.

POTATO CHITTING

Seed potatoes or 'sets' are actually tubers about the size of a hen's egg. You can use your own potatoes left over from the maincrop, provided you are certain that they are free of virus and fungus disease, or you can buy in certified seed.

To help them to get an early start in the ground, sets can be put to sprout, or 'chit', in advance of planting. Egg cartons are convenient containers, putting the sets in rose-end up (that is, the end opposite to the one attached to the root). Put the cartons in a cool, light place free from frost and the dormant 'eyes' will develop shoots, which should be short and sturdy and about 2.5cm (1in) long when planted.

This takes about six weeks, so early crops should be started at the beginning of February for planting at the end of March, and maincrops two or three weeks later for planting in April. For earlies, rub off all but two or three shoots before planting, as this will result in large tubers; but for maincrops, leave them all on, except the weakest and smallest.

the fingers, round the sides and in the corners first, finishing in the centre. The same technique applies to peat or similar composts, but much less firming is needed, otherwise they lose their good aeration and drainage qualities. Use a patter to level the surface, and leave the container in a tray of water to moisten the compost thoroughly. If you water after sowing, the seed is likely to be washed into groups, or washed down too deep.

When wooden seed-trays and soil-based composts were used in the past, crocks (pieces of clay pot) were placed over the cracks in the base of the tray for drainage. This can still be done for plants with a greater-than-average need for a well-drained growing medium.

Seeds are sown in containers because they are precious; every one counts, hence the need for particularly careful container preparation and subsequent sowing.

Depending on the size of the seeds, they can be sown either singly in lines, or scattered. In both cases they should be spaced as evenly as possible, so that no seedling runs short of light, room, water or food; crowded seedlings become leggy and weak. Small seeds are all too easily sown in clusters, but by mixing them with a little silver sand they become easier to manage, whether you are trickling the mixture from the palm of your hand or sowing from between thumb and forefinger.

After sowing the seeds, cover with a light sifting of compost, if you know this to be necessary. And for all seeds, stretch clingfilm over the sides and ends of the container to prevent moisture from escaping and to protect the newly sown seeds. Put the container in the appropriate temperature and in a light, but not sunny, place; otherwise the seeds could become too warm.

Look at the seeds every day – the light-excluding covering or clingfilm can be removed, if present. Keep the seedlings out of direct sun, to prevent their leaves from being scorched, and keep them well supplied with water.

CHAPTER FIVE

THE SENSITIVE PLANT

The way that plants respond to the light is more sophisticated than we imagine. Among the many plants that have a noticeable response are sunflowers (Helianthus sp., LEFT), which turn their heads to follow the sun, and evening primroses (Oenothera sp., BELOW), which have a definite clock that enables them to open their flowers in the evening, when they are pollinated by moths.

THE EFFECTS OF LIGHT

If you looked closely at the plants in your garden, you would notice that not only is there an annual change – with new shoots emerging in spring, buds and flowers forming in spring and summer, fruit forming and leaves dying in autumn, and the plant closing down into dormancy in winter – but there are also differences within any 24-hour day. The plant has quite clear-cut rhythms during those 24 hours, so that you can actually see changes in the way that leaves and flowers behave, and in their appearance. This daily rhythm is affected by variations in the degree of light, in temperature and humidity, and by the effect of night and day. Plants are, in fact, far more sensitive than we often realize. Although they cannot move about, as we do, this does not mean that they do not respond to external stimuli.

They are highly responsive to light and gravitational stimuli. You can see this in the way a plant will curve as it grows towards the sun. Take the wood sorrel, *Oxalis acetosella*, for example. You will see that its leaves close in the evening with a downward movement. So, too, do those of the false acacia (*Robinia pseudoacacia*); while those of the wattle (*Acacia locantha*) go the opposite way, and close upwards, as do clover (*Trifolium* sp.) leaves. If you wander around the garden in the evening in spring you will find that anemones (*Anemone* sp.) close up their flowers for the night, and so do celandines (*Ranunculus ficaria*). Crocuses (*Crocus* sp.) and winter aconites (*Eranthis hyemalis*) close too. The following morning, if it is a sunny day, all those flowers will be open again.

Flowers respond to a very definite clock, opening in the morning between 8 and 9 a.m. and closing up between 5 and 6 p.m. The hotter the temperature, the earlier the flowers open and the later they close. If the day is cold and cloudy, some will stay shut all day, unless you cheat and bring them into a warm room, where they will open up.

As far as plants being affected by light are concerned, the sunflower (*Helianthus* sp.) is perhaps the best-known example (its name in French, *tournesol*, literally means 'turn sun'). Sunflowers, along with several other plants in the *Compositae* family, have flower heads that bend with the angle of the sun's rays; once the sun has set, the flower head returns to the upright and bends back to the east again, ready to face the morning sun. The whole movement is probably influenced by growth hormones, which are concentrated on the shadier side of the plant, so that the flower head bends towards the light. After dark, the illuminated side (on which growth during the day was slower) catches up and the stem straightens out again. Other plants, which are pollinated by night-flying moths, close in the daytime and open at night.

SUNDIAL PLANTS

The great Swedish naturalist Carolus Linnaeus (1707–78) described how flowers could be used as a form of colourful sundial.

At 4 a.m. the morning-glory (*Ipomoea* sp.) trumpets the dawn; at 5 a.m. *Cistus* spirals open; at 6 a.m. the day lily (*Hemerocallis* sp.) opens, so called because its flowers last for one day only. The wood sorrel (*Oxalis*) petals flex outwards at 9 a.m. At midday the passion flower (*Passiflora caerulea*) displays its floral pyrotechnics. Later in the day, the sepals of the evening primrose burst open at 6 p.m. Like the day lilies, they have only a brief life.

In the nineteenth century, J. C. Loudon also listed plants (see below) for the Victorian conceit of a 'clock' bed, divided into segments to relate to the hours of the day, in which the plants were supposed to open at the appropriate times. Nature being what it is, they did not always oblige.

DIAL PLANTS
(from J. C. Loudon, Encyclopedia of Gardening, 1822)

Species	Opens in the morning at		Shut from noon to night		Species	Opens in the morning at		Shut from noon to night	
	Hours	Mins.	Hours	Mins.		Hours	Mins.	Hours	Mins.
Tragopogon luteum	3	5	9	10	Hypochæris maculata	6	7	4	5
Leontodon serotinum	4	0	12	1	Nymphaea alba	7	0	5	0
Picris echioides	4	5	12	0	Lactuca sativa	7	0	10	0
Crepis alpina	4	5	12	0	Tagetes erecta	7	0	3	4
Chicorium intybus	4	5	8	9	Anagallis arvensis	7	8	2	3
Papaver nudicaule	5	0	7	0	Hieracium pilosella	8	0	2	0
Hemerocallis fulva	5	0	7	8	Dianthus prolifer	8	0	1	0
Sonchus laevis	5	0	11	12	Calendula arvensis	9	0	3	0
S. alpinus	5	0	12	0	Arenaria purpurea	9	10	2	3
Convolvulus arvensis	5	6	4	5	Portulaca hortensis	9	10	11	12
Lapsana communis	5	6	10	0	Malva caroliniana	9	10	12	1
Leontodon Taraxacum	5	6	8	9	Stellaria media	9	10	9	10

RESPONSES TO LIGHT

Although seemingly motionless to the eye, plants can be seen – using time-lapse photography – to respond to their environment in all sorts of secret ways.

Below ground, the primary root of a germinating plant will thrust downwards, reacting positively to the Earth's gravitational pull. Above ground, if a young plant is laid on its side, the reverse happens, and the stem turns up, away from the pull of gravity, towards the light. The means by which it does so are growth hormones, called auxins, which accumulate on the shadier side of the stem, elongating it, so that it turns towards the light.

Once the stem is vertical, growth returns to its normal uniform pattern. The growth hormones are produced in the growing tip near the stem apex and, besides regulating growth, they also suppress dormant buds lower down the stem (see page 129).

If a plant is illuminated directly from above, the stem will grow vertically upwards, but if the light source is moved 90 degrees to the side, the response is immediate, and the plant bends towards the light. Leaves and leaf stalks are adapted to make the most of the light. The stems of some leaves – the petioles – will orientate the leaf blades so that the maximum amount of light is gathered.

Leaf, and even petal, movements also depend on the quantity of light available. If a time-lapse camera recorded a 24-hour period and this was compressed into a few seconds of viewing time, you would see what appeared to be a remarkable ballet of leaves, as they move in response to the light. Botanists call these rhythms 'sleep movements' and the different species of plant respond in various ways. Leaves held horizontally during the day will often droop after dark, only to be raised again at sunrise the following day. Flowers respond in a similar way, their opening and closing caused by expansion of the cells on the petal's upper surface, forcing the petal to open. In closure, the reverse occurs and the lower cells increase in size. This differential expansion of the cells is caused by the uptake of water.

GOOD PLANTS FOR SHADE
Acanthus mollis
Ajuga
Bergenia
Brunnera
Digitalis
Epimedium
Euphorbia robbiae
Hosta
Lamium
Pachysandra
Polygonatum
Symphytum
Vinca

DAY-LENGTH MANIPULATION

One of the most interesting aspects of plant growth is the way in which the plant adapts to periods of light and dark. This response was discovered in the 1920s by W. W. Gardner and H. A. Allard, and was termed photoperiodism. Plants can flower only when they have reached a size sufficient to support the weight of blossom and fruit and have sufficient food reserves to supply the needs of reproduction (rather in the same way that teenage girls do not attain puberty until they have passed a specific weight). Plants use their leaves to determine the passage of time and set in train reproduction, by measuring the amount of daylight in each 24-hour period. Some plants will flower only when daylight hours are below a certain level, and others only when they are higher. Short-day plants are those that need fewer than a certain number of hours of daylight per day. Long-day plants require the opposite. Chrysanthemums start to flower when day lengths drop

WHAT IS LIGHT?

Light is the manifestation of energy in the form of wave motion, producing effects of light, warmth and sound, depending on the length of the waves. The waves that we sense as red light are longer than those that give us yellow light, and still longer than those that create the effect of blue light. Ultra-violet light rays are just too short for us to be able to perceive them as light, and infra-red rays are too long to be perceived by the human eye, although they will actually produce an image on a photographic plate. When we receive a great number of light waves, we do not separate out the individual colours but perceive the whole spectrum as bright white light. This spectrum is the same as that of the rainbow. Plants are capable of using the red and blue portions of the spectrum for their supply of energy, and they can be grown in artificial light, provided that these particular rays are provided in the light source.

THE BEST INDOOR PLANT FOR SHADE

Known popularly as the cast-iron plant, the aspidistra (*Aspidistra* sp.) originates from the forest floor of Japan, where very little light ever reaches its leaves. Aspidistras were extremely popular in Victorian times, when their ability to withstand the dark gloom of front parlours, coupled with the pollution from coal fires and gas mantles, made them *de rigueur* in almost every front room in Britain.

The aspidistra's tough leathery leaves are almost indestructible, although overwatering may cause brown leaf-spotting. The plant thrives on sympathetic neglect and may reward you with a display of muddy purple flowers, very low down on the plant, about once in every seven years. Do not re-pot the aspidistra too often – once every five years is enough.

It will grow to about 45cm (18in) tall and about 90cm (3ft) wide. *Aspidistra elatior* is very resistant to all forms of pollution. A variegated version (*A. elatior* 'Variegata') has leaves that are spotted and striped with cream.

to below fifteen hours a day; gypsophila flowers when day lengths are longer than fifteen hours.

This knowledge has been extensively used by commercial growers to induce flowering in certain types of plant, using artificial light to increase natural day length, and blinds to simulate short day lengths, so that you can obtain florists' chrysanthemums all year round, and poinsettias (*Euphorbia pulcherrima*) can be induced to flower in time for Christmas, for example.

RIGHT *Although it is the bracts that actually turn scarlet – the true flowers are tiny and yellow –* poinsettias (Euphorbia pulcherrima) *will flower for Christmas, if the plants are given 14 hours of darkness during the autumn and are then returned to prevailing day lengths.*

GROWING UNDER GLASS

The greatest greenhouse ever built was the one designed by Joseph Paxton, the Duke of Devonshire's gardener, to house the Great Exhibition in 1855. It was known, thereafter, as the Crystal Palace.

Greenhouses became popular in the nineteenth century, with the great wealth of plants brought to Britain from the tropics by plant-hunters. The vogue for plant-hunting had started with John Tradescant in the seventeenth century, but the mass production of glass during the Industrial Revolution made it possible for the wealthy to build their own glasshouses, and it became fashionable to compete to house collections of rare species of plants.

Today gardeners still enjoy the benefits of growing exotic plants under glass, either in the greenhouse or in the conservatory. The glass cuts out the ultra-violet light – which is of no apparent benefit to the plant – but allows the infra-red rays through. However, any dirt on the glass greatly cuts down the passage of light.

It is important for the gardener with a greenhouse to realize that he takes over responsibility from nature for almost all the plants' needs. Control of the greenhouse environment is therefore of paramount importance in the plants' survival – not only in terms of light, but of watering and nutrients as well. As a result, greenhouses are very labour-intensive, as the plants demand regular attention. The single most important point to understand is that, although tropical plants need warmth to survive, they also need humidity. Without watering, proper ventilation and shading, greenhouses can rapidly become plant mortuaries. Fortunately for the gardener, there are now various automatic watering and ventilation systems in mass production, which cut down the gardener's tasks.

The great advantages of a greenhouse are that you can overwinter plants that would die in a temperate climate, grow from seed in warm, light conditions and bring plants into flower early. For the gardener, a greenhouse greatly increases the range of plants that can be grown.

PLANTS SUITABLE FOR GROWING IN GREENHOUSES		
Anthurium andreanum	Ficus benjamina	Phoenix roebelinii
Caladium candidum	Hibiscus rosa-sinensis	Schlumbergera gaertneri
Clianthus puniceus	Hoya australis	Trachelospermum
Cymbidium orchids	Lapageria rosea	jasminoides
Datura suaveolens	Neoregelia carolinae	'Variegata'
Dizygotheca elegantissima	'Tricolor'	Zygocactus truncatus

PLANTS SUITABLE FOR GROWING UNDER CLOCHES AND COLD FRAMES
Beans, broad, French, kidney
Celery
Chrysanthemums
Corn (sweet corn or maize)
Cucumbers
Daffodils and narcissus
Lettuce
Melons
Onions
Peas
Radish
Strawberries

RIGHT *Greenhouses, with just a little warmth, are a great boon for gardeners, allowing them to grow plants that would otherwise perish in the winter in temperate climates. And a simple cold frame provides enough protection to extend the growing season of plants by a couple of weeks at either end.*

CLOCHES AND COLD FRAMES

Cloches and cold frames provide similar advantages to the greenhouse but on a smaller scale. They allow the gardener to extend the growing season and protect plants from extremes of climate that might otherwise prevent them from ripening or maturing properly. Because the temperature under a cloche or cold frame is higher than that outside, the growing season may be extended by a couple of weeks at either end, getting any early vegetables off to a good start.

Cloches are useful because they are portable and can be moved around at will, wherever they are needed. They come in various forms – glass or plastic, squares, tunnels, etc. They need to be removed to water the plants, since they prevent moisture from reaching the soil. Ideally, the ends should be sealed as well, to prevent wind tunnels from being created.

Cold frames perform a similar function and can be made from a simple wooden box with a sheet of clear plastic over the top.

MOVEMENT

In their efforts to become upwardly mobile, plants are supported by a range of structures. In the case of ivy, for example, by aerial adventitious roots; in clematis, by leaf petioles; and in briony, by grasping and spiralling tendrils (see diagrams below).

Those plants that grow spirally round a support are called twiners. Among them are honeysuckle (*Lonicera periclymenum*) and Brazilian firecracker (*Manettia inflata*), both of which twine clockwise, and the fountain flower (*Ceropegia sandersonii*) and wisteria (*Wisteria sinensis*), which twine anticlockwise. The tips of twiners grow in wide circles to give them a better chance of coming into contact with the support (see right). In the passion flower (*Passiflora caerulea*), the tendrils that it uses to support itself are very sensitive to touch. Differential growth in the tendrils spring-loads the climber, so that it is pulled back into place if the wind tears it away from its support.

When providing support for climbing plants, remember that, with a full load of leaves and flowers, plants become quite heavy. If it is not properly secured, very lightweight trellis will blow down, when heavily laden, in high winds, so make sure that it is anchored firmly in the ground.

Plants that simply scramble, such as roses and other prickly plants, will need some assistance if they are to stay attached to vertical surfaces, and should be tied at intervals with plastic ties to wires or trellis. However, if you grow them through other plants (an attractive way of extending the flowering season), you can often dispense with supports.

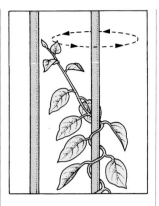

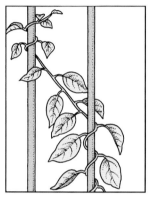

ABOVE *Climbers that twine around a support describe large circles with their tips, some genera twining clockwise, others anticlockwise.*

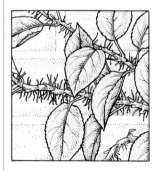

AERIAL ROOTS
Plants with aerial roots are self-clinging, the fine roots have sucker-like pads at their tips to let them grip any surface.

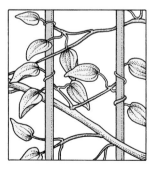

LEAF PETIOLES
Many climbers, such as most forms of clematis, climb using the stalks – or petioles – of their leaves to support themselves.

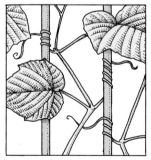

COILING TENDRILS
Some plants produce independent tendrils specifically for the purpose of support. These are naturally spring-loaded.

TWINING STEMS
In some plants, such as runner beans, the whole stem moves in wide circles, in its attempt to find a support to cling to.

RIGHT *Clematis 'Niobe', like all other forms of clematis, needs a support to grow against. Clematis climbs using either its leaf stalks or tendrils, depending on the species.*

BELOW *Runner beans, which climb by twining themselves around a support, need a good open framework of canes to allow the maximum light and air to develop the flowers and then the seeds. Either a double row of canes tied together at the top, or a similarly tied wigwam, is ideal. Lining the trench with newspaper helps to retain moisture in the soil.*

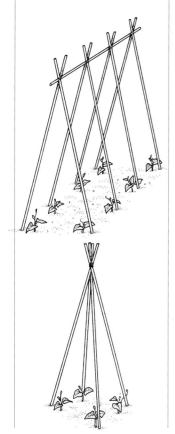

SUPPORTS FOR RUNNER BEANS

When planting runner beans you need to provide an efficient support system, either of rows or a wigwam of canes, tied together at their tips. Make sure that the base of each cane is firmly embedded in the soil.

SUPPORTING CLIMBERS ON A WALL

If you are fixing a trellis to a wall, it pays to use hooks and hinges, so that the whole trellis panel can be lowered carefully to the ground when the wall is being repainted. Fix the trellis a couple of inches from the wall, using battens, to allow air to circulate.

CLIMBERS AND HOW THEY SUPPORT THEMSELVES

Twining stems	Tendrils and sucker pads	Aerial roots
Actinidia kolomikta	*Ampelopsis*	*Asteranthera ovata*
Aristolochia elegans	*brevipedunculata*	*Campsis × tagliabuana*
Celastrus orbiculatus	'Elegans'	'Mme Galen'
Humulus lupulus	*Bryonia alba*	*Epipremnum pictum*
'Aureus'	*Cissus antarctica*	*Hedera colchica*
Lonicera japonica	*Clematis montana* cvs	'Dentata Variegata'
'Auroereticulata'	*Cobaea scandens*	*Hoya carnosa*
Menispermum canadense	*Eccremocarpus scaber*	*Hydrangea petiolaris*
Mina lobata	*Lathyrus odoratus*	*Monstera deliciosa*
Parthenocissus	*Parthenocissus*	*Philodendron scandens*
tricuspidata	*tricuspidata*	*Pileostegia viburnoides*
Tropaeolum tuberosum	*Passiflora caerulea*	*Schizophragma*
Wisteria floribunda cvs	*Vitis coignetiae*	*integrifolium*

TOUCH

Some plants are responsive to touch. The fascinating water plant, *Neptunia* – a member of the *Acacia* family collected by botanists for the Royal Botanic Gardens at Kew a few years ago – is particularly sensitive to touch, even to water droplets, at which its leaves quickly start to fold up. In the Palm House at Kew, another plant from South America, *Nemosa* (or the 'sensitive plant', as it is sometimes called), has an even greater sensitivity to touch. A native to the tropics, and often kept as a house plant in Britain, it quickly folds up each leaflet if you touch it – its folding mechanism brought about by cells at the base of each leaflet acting like a hinge. If you run your finger down the whole leaf, that too starts to close, and if a more major stimulus, such as that provided by a feeding animal, is experienced, all the leaves on the plant start to fold up. The messages are passed from cell to cell in the plant, rather in the same way that messages are transmitted by the nervous system in humans.

Touch has been put to use by scientists in experiments to breed healthier, stronger plants. If you had two plants, one on a windowsill outside the house and one indoors, you would find that the one inside became weaker and more leggy. Although you might be excused for thinking that this was all due to lack of light, this is not actually the reason. The difference in the level of light reaching the plants in these conditions is minimal, but the plant outside is subjected to stress, as its branches blow about in the wind, whereas the one indoors remains stationary. The exposure to stress actually benefits the plant, building a shorter, stronger specimen. This can be tested if you plant two identical subjects, such as beans, and stroke one of the young plants for a few minutes each day. The stroked plant will respond by becoming shorter and stronger than the unstroked plant.

Touch is, in the end, only a form of vibration. If touch is beneficial, then perhaps talking to plants is not as daft as it seems. Sound is, after all, just another form of vibration.

INSECTIVOROUS PLANTS

Charles Darwin was fascinated by insectivorous plants. There are well over 1,000 plants that show movement in response to touch, but those with which we are most familiar are the insectivorous plants like the sundew (*Drosera* sp.). This has thousands of hairs on the surface of its leaves, and each of those hairs, when touched, moves. That movement ensnares the insect on the surface of the leaf and shuffles it into the centre, where it can be digested more successfully. Even more dramatic movement can be seen in the Venus flytrap (*Dionaea muscipula*). On the upper surfaces of its leaves are tiny hairs, which are sensitive to touch. If the insect touches the hairs, they respond. The stimulation of one hair is insufficient to cause the flytrap to close, because otherwise it would close every time rain droplets fell, but if the same hair is stimulated twice in rapid succession, it closes in two stages – partly the first time, and more firmly the second time.

Once the stimulation has taken place, the message is passed down to the hinge cells. Darwin investigated the response and showed that there was some kind of electrical activity on the surface of the leaf, which stimulated the closure. But in the last 10 years scientists have investigated this in detail, and it now appears that it is similar to the human nervous system, consisting of a wave of electrochemical stimuli between cells. It differs from an animal system in that it is a much slower response, going from cell to cell rather than down nerve fibres. It controls only one activity – the closing of the leaf – and not a whole range of activities, as it does in animals.

RIGHT *The Venus flytrap* (Dionaea muscipula) *gets its source of nitrogen from insects which it traps in its evergreen hinged leaves, each one edged with stiff bristles to ensure that the insect, once trapped, remains a prisoner until it can be digested.*

CHAPTER SIX
SHAPING PLANTS

I n a winter landscape you can clearly see each broad-leaved tree's own unique shape, a silhouette as individual as a fingerprint – oaks with their massive limbs, the tracery of silver birch, the slender columns of black poplars and the elegant, weeping, waterside willows – each with its own genetic branch print. Evergreens, too, have their own distinct outline, such as that of the unmistakable cedar of Lebanon

Different genera of plants have their own individual genetic make-up that determines their character and appearance, which can be seen most clearly in their bare winter outlines (LEFT). However, both man and nature can wreak changes in these outlines through pruning. In nature's case, this is often done by the wind, which has stunted the growth of these birch trees (BELOW) on the windward side.

SOME TYPICAL OUTLINES OF ENGLISH NATIVE TREES

The outlines below are those of some of the more familiar trees, as you would expect to see them growing in the countryside. Occasionally, however, prevailing winds or the effects of salt spray from the sea modify the shape that nature intended. Buds fail to form on the exposed side of the tree, with consequent imbalanced growth. The form of the plants is fixed in the cells contained in the seed (see page 96).

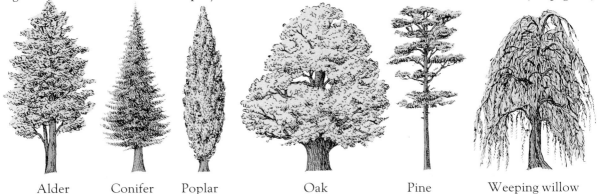

Alder   Conifer   Poplar   Oak   Pine   Weeping willow

(*Cedrus libani*), with its characteristic spreading umbrella of inky-green, needle-like leaves.

But the natural shape of plants can be altered by a number of factors, not just their loss of leaves. Animals and climate both play a part – animals browse on the branches; strong winds on exposed hillsides and salt spray on seaside cliffs distort the shape that nature intended for the tree or shrub, as the tender shoots get cut off before they reach their prime.

Plants, like man, suffer from exposure, but it has been man, more than nature, who has been responsible for most of the changes to the plant's natural shape that we see in our gardens – the art of clipping trees into geometric shapes, known as topiary, being one of the most obvious examples. And in the countryside, a range of ancient crafts attests to man's skill in shaping nature – laying hedges to keep stock enclosed, coppicing lime and beech to create plentiful supplies of young wood, and pollarding willows to keep the new shoots out of reach of browsing animals and to provide supple young shoots for baskets.

Some environments are notably more extreme than others, with consequent drastic effects on plants. In the Burren, south of Galway Bay in Ireland, the wind and spray act like a razor, severing any shoots that dare raise themselves above the limestone kerb. Every year the shoots are pruned by nature, meristems (see page 48) and shoot tips are destroyed, but new juvenile growth appears regularly each spring, fortunately, on even the most gnarled and ancient plants, particularly on the leeward side.

THE APICAL BUD

Ask the average gardener why he or she prunes a plant, and you will probably get the following answers: to control unwanted growth, to get rid of dead or diseased wood, or to stimulate the formation of flowers or fruit. But, in the latter case, not many gardeners would be able to tell you *why* pruning has this effect.

In order to acquire a proper understanding of how to prune plants, you need to know what causes the growth to take place in the way it does. Knowledge of this has enabled man to shape plants to his taste in a myriad of ways – in commercial circumstances, to produce flowers of particular kinds, to increase the yield of certain crops, to create a multi-stemmed plant from a single tree, and to carve out elaborate topiary forms from evergreens.

How does the plant actually grow? Each plant forms new tissues in areas of active cell division called the meristem, which are found near the tips of both root and shoot. Meristem growth ensures that the leaves are quickly elevated into the sunlight. The same process applies to roots, ensuring that they penetrate deeply into the soil (see page 48). When stems and roots have gained a moderate height and length, they begin to thicken, to give stability and support to the plant. The stem's growing tip, known as the apical bud, is much more complex than that of the root, both in structure and activity.

In the example shown below, the cells of the apical meristem are highly magnified. The nucleus of each cell contains the chromosomes.

RIGHT *This greatly magnified photograph of the apical meristem of a sycamore shoot shows the apical bud (in the centre of the picture) surrounded by axillary leaf buds.*

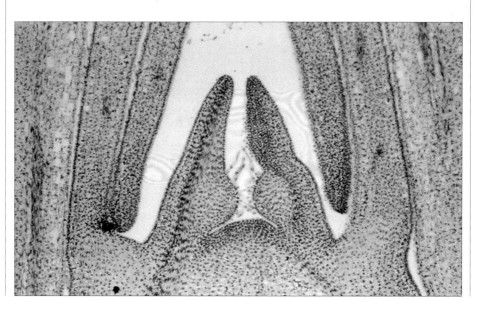

Chromosomes are strand-like structures contained in every cell, which hold the genetic code of the plant and are responsible for the transfer of hereditary characteristics from cell to cell, as the plant grows and enlarges (and ultimately from plant to plant through cross-pollination). They are divided so that each pair of new cells holds an identical set of genetic information. The meristem also produces the growth hormone

LEFT *Chrysanthemums in florists' shops are typical examples of man's interference with nature. In this large single chrysanthemum, a medium incurved form known as 'John Hughes', the secondary buds have been pinched out to concentrate all the energy in the apical bud, to produce this outsize bloom.*

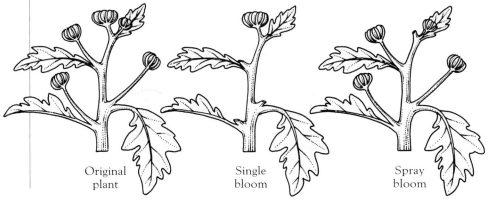

Original plant

Single bloom

Spray bloom

LEFT *The process of budding and disbudding. The original plant (far left) has both an apical bud at the top and secondary buds. Removing the secondary bud (centre) concentrates all the growing hormones in the top, apical bud; removing the apical buds (left) sends the same hormones down the plant to the secondary buds, to develop an even-sized spray of flowers.*

RIGHT *In the spray
chrysanthemum 'Deep
Rytang', the grower has
removed the apical bud, so
that all the secondary buds
develop at the same time,
to produce a very even-
sized spray.*

called auxin, which not only promotes cell division, but diffuses
downwards and inhibits the development of resting lateral buds,
which otherwise would compete with the apical bud for nutrients and
light. The removal of the apical bud and its suppressive hormone
allows the dormant lateral buds lower down to develop. In a very short
time, the buds between the leaf stalk and the stem (called axillary buds)
produce shoots that compete to become the new lead growth. In this
way, plants respond to any damage to the growing tip.

In the world of commercial horticulture, growers have used the
plant's hormonal response to damage on a huge scale. Take chrysanthemums (*Chrysanthemum* sp.), for example. Left to its own devices,
each chrysanthemum will form flower buds, its primary function
being to produce flowers, in order to provide seeds to reproduce itself.
The crown bud is the one that is going to get there first – a version of
the survival of the fittest – because the hormone produced in the apical
meristem is going to inhibit the growth of competitors. Growers help
nature by removing the smaller axillary buds, so that all the energy is
concentrated in the crown bud, producing massive blooms that create
the huge, mop-headed chrysanthemums seen in florists' shops. Another version of the chrysanthemum, which is also popular with

CREATING A STANDARD FUCHSIA

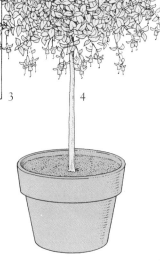

1   2   3   4

1 When the fuchsia is about 15cm (6in) tall, pinch out any side shoots that appear in the axils of the leaves. Do not pinch out the side stems, as the plant needs these leaves to survive.
2 When a fairly tall, straight stem is reached, of the required height, pinch out the crown bud or top shoot.
3 As the new side shoots form at the top of the stem, pinch them out at their tips to encourage the top to become bushy.
4 Once the fuchsia has formed a good ball shape at the top of the plant, the leaves lower down on the stem will eventually drop off. If they do not do so, you should pinch them out yourself.

CREATING A BUSH FUCHSIA

This is virtually the opposite procedure to that involved in creating a standard fuchsia.

When the cutting has three sets of leaves, pinch out the growing tip. Then, when the side shoots have developed, pinch out the tips of these as well. Continue to pinch out the growing points of the new side shoots until the plant has reached a good bushy shape with evenly spaced shoots.

flower-arrangers, is the spray chrysanthemum. This, too, would not appear in our shops if the plant was left to its own devices. You would naturally get one larger-than-average flower and a number of smaller ones. To create the even-sized spray that arrangers like, growers remove the crown bud, which then permits the growth hormone to be diverted to the axillary buds, which form together at the same time.

A similar system operates when you want to make plants become bushier. If you pinch out the tip (or apical bud), the hormone diverts to the axillary buds, and the plant's energy is also diverted. This principle is widely used in vegetable production, on tomatoes and runner beans, for example.

The principles of apical dominance are also used to create standard and bush fuchsias (*Fuchsia* sp.) by removing either the crown bud or the lateral buds, depending on which form you are aiming to create. To propagate fuchsias, simply use the growing points of tips you have pinched out as cuttings (see page 79), as they grow easily from these.

POLLARDING AND COPPICING

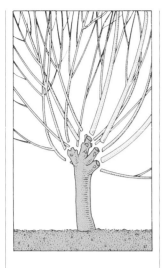

ABOVE *The art of pollarding, in which the new season's shoots are cut back to the main stem, is practised in willows to produce a thicker crop of slender shoots for use in basket-making.*

BELOW *Coppicing has the same effect. In dogwoods (*Cornus sp.*), some of which have beautiful young red shoots, this is done for ornamental purposes.*

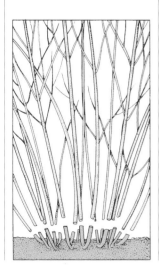

Single-stemmed plants can be pruned to produce multi-stemmed ones, using the same principle of apical dominance. In other words, you cut back the leading shoots, which allows secondary shoots to develop.

The eucalyptus tree (*Eucalyptus* sp.), a native of Australia and Tasmania, is a good example. People prefer the shape of the rounded leaves on its juvenile growth to the more slender, elongated leaves on the adult plant. Another advantage of severe pruning is that you get a white, waxy coating on the bark, which many people, particularly flower-arrangers, find attractive. Yet another advantage is that it keeps the plant in check. A fully mature tree would be far too large for most small city plots.

Growing as it does in Australia, where bush fires are frequent hazards, the eucalyptus has adapted to its environment and can regenerate itself when cut down to base level, either by fire or by the gardener's shears. In fact, eucalyptus trees in Britain sometimes get cut down to ground level in hard winters, and many gardeners make the mistake of ripping them out, when they should have left nature to do its work, in which case the eucalyptus would probably produce a multi-stemmed plant in its place.

Many gardeners are nervous about cutting plants back hard, but, as far as the eucalyptus is concerned, this presents no problem. Within about three months of hard pruning, the dormant buds will have sprung to life and shoots will be sprouting around the clump. By autumn, a new plant will have been regenerated.

Another plant that can similarly be regenerated is the lime tree (*Tilia platyphyllos*) and the method used to regenerate young plants from old is known as coppicing. In one small coppice of lime, which has existed for over 2,000 years, a single tree has now produced more than 80 stems. Normally a lime tree would not live for anything like 2,000 years; you would be lucky to get 250 years out of it. But repeatedly cutting down, or coppicing, the tree allows a continual supply of new growth. If you do not coppice lime, it is likely to split, so it is an ideal candidate for this technique.

Some trees and shrubs produce new growth that is much more colourful than mature bark; if the shoots age, the colour fades and darkens. Bright effects for the winter garden can be created by hard pruning of dogwoods (*Cornus alba*) and ornamental bramble (*Rubus* sp.), for example. When pruning any plant, you need to be aware of both its

LEFT Coppicing is a countryside craft that has been practised for thousands of years. Cutting beech trees down to the base produces a multi-stemmed plant instead of a single trunk.

BELOW When pruning wood that is thicker than about 2.5cm (1in) in diameter, you will need to use a pruning saw or long-handled loppers rather than secateurs. The aim is to ensure that you do not tear the bark.

First make a cut some distance outwards from the final intended cut, so that the bulk of the weight of the branch is removed.

To remove the branch, undercut it as shown just above the collar (where it joins the main stem), then make the final cut just outside the collar, angling it slightly so that the base of the cut is slightly further from the trunk than the top.

growth habit, and whether the buds grow in opposite or alternate pairs (see page 137).

When pruning dogwoods for autumn colour, the aim is to obtain the best supply of new growth. You prune the plant in spring, just when the buds are coming out of dormancy. Once the plant has recovered from the initial shock, when nothing visibly seems to be happening, you will suddenly get quite dramatic vigorous growth. After three months you should get about a metre of extension growth, so you will have plenty of stems for good winter colour.

TOPIARY

Topiary – the formal pruning and training of plants into geometric shapes – is yet another area where the gardener manipulates the purposes of nature for his own ends. Topiary has been practised since Roman times. You either love it or you loathe it, but either way the skill involved is undeniable, not only in the clipping but also in the growing, since it is not particularly easy to get the plants to grow evenly and well.

One of the most important factors in achieving good topiary shapes is that the plants must receive adequate supplies of sunshine on all sides. The siting of any piece of topiary is therefore one of your first considerations. The best growth will always be on the south side, and the worst on the north side. Shelter from overhanging trees will cause topiary pieces to lean towards the light, giving them a curiously drunken appearance.

Anyone who has a hedge in their garden that needs clipping is probably aware of the problem of overshadowing. If you are not careful and clip the base of the hedge harder than the top, you create an overhang,

RIGHT *Nowhere is the gardener's control of nature more evident than in the art of topiary, where the natural shape of the plant is contorted, by pruning, into a variety of geometric forms, as here at Haddon Hall in Derbyshire.*

and the top then shades out the bottom more each year, with the result that eventually there will be no leaves at the base of the hedge at all. The same applies to topiary. You should opt for designs that are wider at the base than at the apex, to prevent this from occurring.

PLANTS FOR TOPIARY

Only certain plants can be trained to create a topiary shape – evergreens with small, densely packed leaves, pliable growth and the ability to recover quickly from clipping. Box (*Buxus sempervirens* cvs) and yew (*Taxus baccata*) are the best subjects, because they create a dense, strong mass of leaves and are slow-growing, which means that you do not have to clip the shapes too frequently. Privet (*Ligustrum* sp.), bay (*Laurus nobilis*) and holly (*Ilex* sp.) are also good candidates, although not as neat-looking.

MAINTAINING THE PLANTS

Any plant needs a good start, with plenty of fertilizer, and it should be growing strongly before any clipping is attempted. Although simple geometric shapes can be clipped freehand, larger, more complex shapes require a frame – either for the topiary to be trained around, or

CREATING A TOPIARY PYRAMID

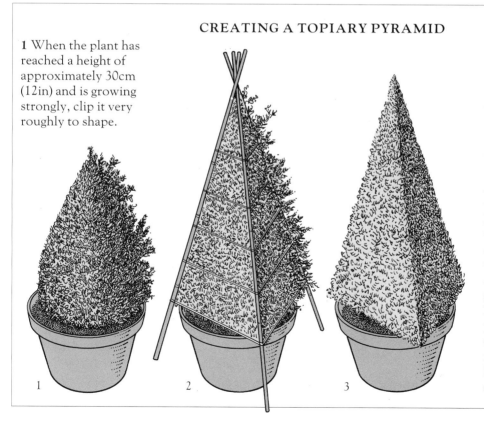

1 When the plant has reached a height of approximately 30cm (12in) and is growing strongly, clip it very roughly to shape.

2 The following year, using a cutting guide made out of three canes bound together with wire placed over the plant, cut the plant again to achieve the desired shape.

3 When the plant reaches the desired height and shape for your garden, clip it every year. Cutting out the leading shoot will ensure that the plant grows no taller. And keeping the size of the plant down with regular clipping will help to make sure that it becomes very bushy and dense.

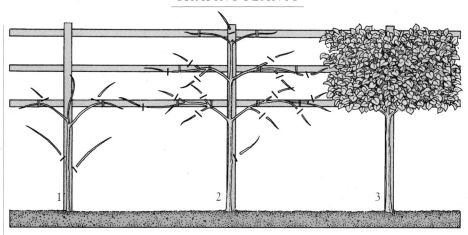

PLEACHING

RIGHT *Create a sturdy frame of stakes and horizontal cross-bars at the required height.*

1 Trim side shoots to last couple of buds on any side shoots from main stem, and when first shoots reach the horizontal cross-bars, tie them in and prune to last two buds.

2 As tree grows, continue to tie in new shoots and prune to last two buds. Cut out growing point when pleached hedge reaches required height.

3 Remove any lower shoots from the main stem to leave it clear.

in the form of a clipping guide – constructed out of chicken wire, or canes and wire.

The cutting will have to be carried out anything from once a year (for yew, which is slow-growing) to twice a year (for box), three times a year (for privet), and even more often, if you want a very neat shape.

You also have to take care not to clip back too far. For instance, a piece of yew should be clipped back to about 3mm (⅛in) of the current year's growth. More than that and you risk cutting into brown wood, without any resting buds, with the result that you will kill off that part of the bush. As with any woody plants, you will also need to prune out any dead or diseased wood at regular intervals.

PLEACHING

Pleaching is similar to topiary, in that once again the gardener manipulates the plant to his design, rather than nature's. But in this case, much of the work is done simply by bending the plants, rather than cutting them, once you have removed the lower-level shoots. After that, you are not so much distorting the plant's natural ability to grow in a particular way as simply training it to grow exactly where you want it to.

Pleached trees are popular as a formal, high-level hedge, in which a wall of neatly clipped, intertwined foliage is created fairly high up on a clear stem. Pleaching is very useful if you want to blot out an unattractive view, but is equally good, in larger gardens, for formal avenues. Hornbeams (*Carpinus betulus*) and limes (*Tilia platyphyllos*) are good subjects, as they grow quickly and respond well to clipping.

The trees are planted out as you would a hedge, but with wider spacing, and a frame is used, to train the branches horizontally.

Pleaching is similar to any other form of pruning, in which damaged or diseased wood is removed, as are any feathers on the stem, or any crossing or unnecessary branches that cannot easily be tied in.

RIGHT *Pleached lime trees forming an avenue at Chatsworth. The same principle, by which the lower branches are removed and the higher ones bent horizontally to join together, can be copied on a far smaller scale to surround a knot garden, perhaps, in a smaller garden.*

SHAPING NATURE FOR CONSERVATION

Some 25 years ago the British countryside was ravaged by the effects of Dutch elm disease, which returned to Britain after an absence of about 300 years. It did such damage that in the south of England few elms survived. The problem was not only that the trees were scattered around the countryside, but that, being so large, it was very difficult to spray them. At Wakehurst Place in Sussex – sister-garden to the Royal Botanic Gardens at Kew – the curator, John Simmons, set about creating a reserve supply of elms that could be kept free from the disease.

How was this achieved? The answer lay in creating a special bank, in hedge form, of all the different elms under threat from the disease, and then in cutting them back frequently to keep them juvenile. Cutting back the trees created plenty of young shoots that rooted easily and thereby added to the supply. Also, by keeping the trees to a manageable height, it would be easier to spray them if the beetles that carry the disease struck again.

RIGHT *The ravages of Dutch elm disease, in which the beetle that transmits the disease burrows into and destroys the bark, eventually killing the tree.*

PRUNING FLOWERING SHRUBS

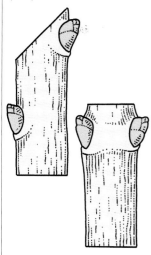

Pruning causes more panic among gardeners than any other task in the garden. For a start, nobody knows exactly what to cut off, or when to cut it off. And since you are told that if you cut off the wood on which next year's flowers will appear, you will have a rather uninteresting plant the following year, it creates endless tension in the average gardener.

Since most gardening techniques have been based on the practices carried out in large gardens, in the days when there were several gardeners and the work had to be organized efficiently, pruning has generally been done at specific times of the year. This need not be the case, however, in a small garden. The gardener, armed with a pair of secateurs, is far better off simply strolling around the garden, removing sections of the plant whenever it is obviously time to do so – in other words, if you are pruning flowering shrubs, prune them just after they have flowered, when you can see what is new wood and what is old (that is, the wood bearing the old withered flowers or seed heads). This will work reasonably well as a general guide, but will not necessarily give you 'show' class quantities or size of bloom. For this you will need to consult a specialist book.

The aim of pruning a flowering shrub is primarily to induce it to produce a good crop of flowers in the next flowering season. It is fairly logical, therefore, to prune it after it has flowered. Not only can you see which parts of the plant to prune out, but you also give the plant the maximum period of time in which to build up its reserves for the following season.

Pruning is also done to improve shape, or to regulate size. So the first thing to do is to remove any dead, damaged or diseased wood. Then cut out any unnecessary or weak shoots. Remember that when you are pruning a plant to improve its shape, you should cut back to an outward-growing bud, as you want the new shoots to grow outwards, not inwards so that they cross over other branches and increase the competition for light.

Another important point is to make the pruning cuts correctly. You need very sharp cutting equipment, so that you do not tear or damage the wood; you also need to make the cut at the right distance from the bud that you wish to develop. If you leave too much stem between the pruning cut and the bud, the stem will wither and may become diseased. On the other hand, if you cut too close to the bud, you may easily damage it.

DEAD-HEADING

Removing dying flowers, before the seed has had a chance to develop, encourages the remaining shoots to flower, because the plant is programmed to produce as much seed as possible in order to regenerate itself the following year. Roses are a good example – dead-heading them not only removes unsightly flowers, but actually stimulates further flowering. Moreover, if you leave the seed pods on the roses, the following year's crop will not be as impressive, because the plant feels that it has done all that is required to produce seed and to ensure the continuation of the species.

There is apparently a seven-year cycle in beech trees (*Fagus sylvatica*), whereby the tree slowly builds up its reserves of carbohydrates and once every seven years produces a bumper crop of seeds. But if the flower buds are damaged by frost in the seventh year, the beech will simply produce its mammoth crop the following year, or the year after that, and then the seven-year cycle starts all over again.

If the gardener plays god by removing the seeds, the plant is tricked into thinking that it has to surpass itself the following year instead and will produce a large crop of flowers or fruit. To prevent the plant from exhausting itself and from running short of the necessary carbohydrates, it will require extra feeding, if you are expecting this sort of performance on an annual basis.

PRUNING CLEMATIS

The pruning of groups of plants such as clematis and roses worries most gardeners. In the clematis group, there are three categories: those that flower on old wood (such as *Clematis montana*), those that flower on new stems from old wood (such as C. 'Naiobe'), and those that flower on completely new growth (such as C. 'Hagley Hybrid'). To get the best results from your clematis you do need to know to which group they belong. As a general rule, however, those that flower before June (that is, on old wood) should not be pruned, those that flower on new shoots from old wood you should simply dead-head, and those that flower on new growth you can cut back hard.

PRUNING ROSES

Roses are among the most popular flowering shrubs and it may therefore be worth while going into a bit more detail about pruning them. Roses that flower on the current year's growth, such as modern shrub roses, need heavy pruning. Those, like climbers and ramblers, that flower on old wood need relatively little pruning, as they flower satisfactorily year after year. Their principal pruning need is the removal of tangled stems, to allow more light and air into the bush and to keep it within check. As already mentioned, roses can be pruned in summer after flowering, except in the case of *Rugosa* roses, where you are hoping to have attractive hips later. These are better pruned in spring.

A good point to bear in mind when pruning roses is that the thorns usually face away from the rose head, or, if not, then straight outwards, at right-angles to the stem. If you work your way down from the tip of the shoot, you will reduce the risk of scratching yourself. In any case, wear strong protective gloves.

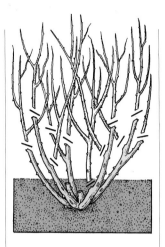

ABOVE *To prune a modern bush rose, cut the rose hard back to a couple of buds on each stem, making the pruning cut just above a bud.*

BELOW *Shrub roses need relatively light pruning, and you should reduce any old woody shoots by about one-third every year. Every other year, cut a few shoots down to the base (these will not flower that year.)*

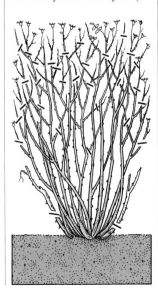

PRUNING MODERN BUSH ROSES

This group includes the large-flowered bush roses (formerly known as hybrid teas), the cluster-flowered bush roses (formerly known as floribundas) and the patio and miniature roses. Pruning back very hard increases the size of the blooms but reduces their number and can also delay flowering by up to three weeks. As a rule of thumb, cut back to about 15–20cm (6–8in), to a couple of good buds on each stem. Remove any crossing stems, or dead or diseased wood. Make the pruning cut just above a bud, as shown left.

PRUNING SHRUB AND OLD ROSES

These need pruning only for cosmetic purposes. It is best to do this in winter for remontants (repeat-flowering roses). Every other year, cut a few of the main stems down to the base, to encourage the growth of new basal shoots. Non-remontant roses can be pruned after flowering, simply thinning them out and reducing old woody shoots by about one-third.

PRUNING CLIMBING AND RAMBLING ROSES

These need very little in the way of pruning, but if you do not wish to have a large, tangled mess to deal with, it is best to train the shoots so that they do not become too entwined. Create a system of horizontal supporting wires, and train any new shoots along these, using rose ties.

True rambler roses flower only once a year, usually in July or August on the growth made the previous season. These stems produce just one crop of flowers. So, ideally, ramblers are pruned immediately after the

---

TYPES OF ROSE

Roses are divided broadly into those categories given here, where a few popular examples in each group are provided. Consult a specialist rose growers' manual for further information.

RAMBLER ROSES	**CLIMBING ROSES**
'American Pillar'	'Albertine'
'Crimson Shower'	'Bantry Bay'
'Dorothy Perkins'	'Casino'
'Easlea's Golden'	'Golden Showers'
'Excelsa'	'Mermaid'
'Sander's White'	'Zéphirine Drouhin'

BUSH ROSES

Large blooms	**Cluster blooms**	**Shrub species**
'Admiral Rodney'	'Amber Queen'	'Agnes'
'Barkarole'	'Debs Delight'	'Jacques Cartier'
'National Trust'	'Golden Years'	*Rosa rugosa*
'Tequila Sunrise'	'Iced Ginger'	*Rosa nitida*
'Tynwald'	'Melody Maker'	*Rosa rubrifolia*
'Valencia'	'Tango'	'William Lobb'

flowers have faded, with the flower-bearing stems being removed as close to ground level as possible. After these old shoots have been removed, the new ones that will bear next year's flowers are tied into position. You will have no difficulty differentiating between the new growth and the old: new growth is usually smooth, pale green in colour and has no branches or dead flowers present on it.

LEFT *Roses come in many forms, from massive climbers to tiny patio roses. The cluster-flowered (formerly known as floribunda) bush rose shown here, Rosa 'Matangi', is a modern rose that fits well into a border. It has a height and spread of about 75cm (2ft 6in) and produces its slightly scented double flowers from summer through to autumn.*

PRUNING TO ENCOURAGE FRUIT

BELOW *Espalier-trained apple trees, like all trained fruit trees, take up relatively little space, crop heavily and have the advantage that the apples are easy to harvest. Developed for commercial purposes, they also suit the small garden, where space is always at a premium and where the training wires can easily be attached to a wall.*

The first point to recognize when pruning a fruit tree is that your main aim is to produce a decent crop of fruit, rather than a tree with abundant, lush-looking foliage. If left to its own devices, nature would also prune the fruit tree, but in a different way. The phenomenon known as June or July drop, when embryonic apples start to fall off the tree, is nature's way of ensuring the survival of the fittest. In fact, if you cut open the apples that have dropped on the ground you would find that they generally have only a couple of seeds in them, whereas those that have stayed on the tree – the survivors – have perhaps four or five seeds.

Although you are usually advised to prune fruit trees in winter, because that is when it suits growers to do so, for the average gardener

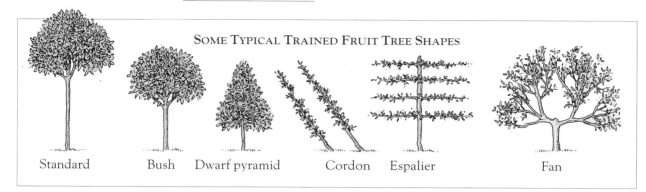

SOME TYPICAL TRAINED FRUIT TREE SHAPES

Standard   Bush   Dwarf pyramid   Cordon Espalier   Fan

it might make more sense to prune the tree when the crop is just forming. That way you preserve the strength of the tree for the production of next year's fruit crop, and for finalizing the current year's crop, although you do have to be careful not to knock the current year's crop off the tree.

Ideally, you should remove one-third of what you think will be next year's flower buds, so that you concentrate the energy in the remaining two-thirds.

The principles of apical dominance are put to good use in training fruit trees, so that they produce not only good crops of fruit, but also the fruit where you want them – and where you can most easily harvest them. For this reason, many fruit trees are these days trained into particular shapes, and they are often grown against walls or in rows along wire supports.

In fact, bending branches also has an effect on growth. When the branches of a tree or shrub are trained horizontally instead of vertically, the plant will try to reach the light, and will therefore make most of its growth on the upper side of these horizontal shoots. The act of bending the branch over also restricts the flow of sap, which in turn puts the plant under pressure and encourages the production of flowers and fruit.

One further trick, which growers sometimes use, is to make a nick in the bark. Again this puts the plant under stress and concentrates its energies on making seed, to continue the reproductive cycle, rewarding the grower with more flowers and fruit on the way.

The main shapes for fruit trees are shown above. They are the classic standard tree, the bush tree, the fan tree and the dwarf pyramid. Espalier and cordon trees are normally trained against wires, fences or walls.

TRAINING A DWARF PYRAMID

To create a dwarf pyramid, initial pruning of the young plant forms the desired conical shape. Immediately after planting, cut back the stem to about 60cm (2ft) above ground level.

By the second winter you need to select half a dozen evenly spaced lower branches and cut them back to about 25cm (10in) long, the last bud being a downward- or outward-facing one. Any other branches at this level should be removed, and branches above it should be cut back to about 15cm (6in), while the tip of the tree is cut back to leave it 30cm (12in) above the top branch.

Each year, in summer, cut the tip of each branch to leave 15cm (6in) of the current year's growth, and cut back any side shoots to 10cm (4in) and secondary shoots to 5cm (2in).

Each winter, cut the leading shoot to leave 20cm (8in) of the previous season's growth. And once the tree has reached the desired size, prune it back twice as hard.

BELOW *Training a dwarf pyramid.*
1 Cut tree back to 60cm (2ft) above ground level.
2 Prune back side shoots in second year after planting, and remove growing tip.
3 Trim in the third year.
4 Cut back the leading shoot each winter.

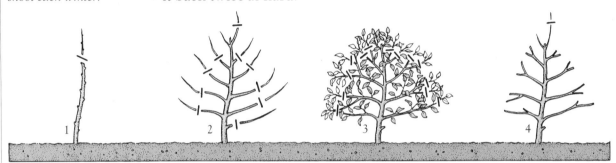

TRAINING A CORDON

Cordons are grown on supporting walls, with wires strung at 60cm (2ft) intervals, or on a post and wire fence. The trees need to be planted at least 90cm (3ft) apart, if you have several of them.

After planting in autumn, cut the leading shoot back to remove one-third of its growth, and cut back any side shoots to a downward-facing bud, with no shoot being more than 8cm (3in) long.

The next summer, prune back the side shoots coming from the main stem to 8cm (3in) and any secondary shoots to half of that. The second winter, prune the leading shoot again to cut off one-third of that year's

RIGHT *Training a cordon.*
1 Cut tree back by one-third in the autumn after planting.
2 Prune back side shoots the following summer.
3 Cut back one-third of the growing point the following winter.
4 Prune the side shoots the following summer.

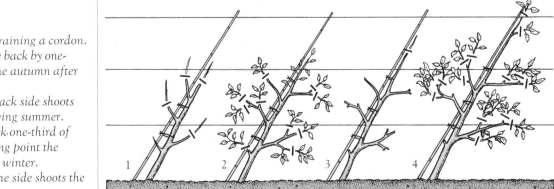

LEFT *Cordon-trained apple trees in a fruit orchard in Kent.*

growth, and in the summer again prune the side shoots and secondary shoots, as before.

Once the tree has reached the desired size, prune the main shoot to 8cm (3in) in summer and the side shoots to 2.5cm (1in).

TRAINING AN ESPALIER

With an espalier, the branches are not only pruned but tied to horizontal supports to create the classic horizontal fanned shape. The wires for the horizontal supports need to be about 60cm (2ft) apart.

ABOVE *A fan-trained fruit tree in a model garden at Chelsea. Fan-training against a south-facing wall is often used for fruit such as peaches and nectarines, which need great exposure to sunshine and the reflected warmth from the wall.*

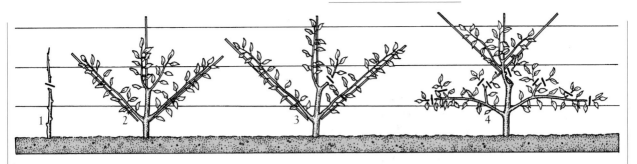

ABOVE Training an espalier.
1 Cut back the tree after planting.
2 Train side shoots the following spring.
3 Cut back side shoots the same summer.
4 Tie in new shoots the following year, and cut back the growth by about one-third.

After planting, prune the main stem to just above the first wire, having first ensured that there are three good buds (to form the side branches) just below the pruning point.

Then, in the spring, train the side shoots on to canes fixed to the wires at a 45-degree angle to the main stem. In the summer, cut the side branches on the main stem back to 8cm (3in).

Next winter, prune the side branches back to remove one-third of the year's growth, and tie them to the first horizontal wire. Prune the main stem as you did in the first year, to within 5cm (2in) of the pruning point, leaving three good buds below the wire.

Carry on repeating the same procedure every year, until the tree forms an upright espalier. Prune the branches as for the cordon each summer and, when the tree is the correct height, cut the growing point of the main stem.

TRAINING A FAN

Fan-trained trees are often grown against a wall, with the intention of using the reflected heat to ripen fruits that might not otherwise ripen in a cool climate. Wires, on which to train the branches, should be fixed to the wall at intervals of 23cm (9in).

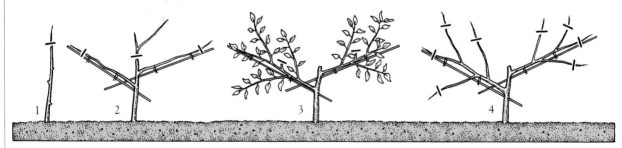

1 After planting, cut back the plant to a strong bud, with at least two buds below this.
2 The second winter, remove the central shoot and prune the side shoots to 45cm (18in). *Tie them to canes that are fixed at an angle of about 45 degrees to the horizontal wire.*
3 Reduce the shoots on each side branch to two on the top and two underneath. *Remove any other buds that now start to appear.*
4 Carry on in this way, tying in the new branches as they become long enough and cutting back new shoots. *In the fourth winter, the plant will be ready to fruit. From now on you should prune the fan in order to produce the best fruit.*

CHAPTER SEVEN

THE NATURAL BALANCE

By autumn the garden is beginning to wind down. Most of the vegetables and fruit have been harvested, and the leaves are beginning to fall as winter dormancy approaches in woody-stemmed trees, shrubs and perennials. Seed heads are bursting and scattering, with the next generation of plants locked inside their embryonic cells.

For the gardener, autumn is the time for preparation – the time to make compost, with plenty of material available for the compost heap, and to dig over the soil, so that the frost can break down the large clods and help to aerate the soil's structure.

As we have seen, the final size and health of a plant are determined to a great extent by the resources available to it. Provided that you, the gardener, return to the soil what you have taken from it, your plants should, by and large, reward you with proper healthy growth. Although not everyone wishes to have an organic garden, once you learn some respect for nature's processes, it seems by far the most sensible line of approach, hence the emphasis placed on it here.

To sustain an organic garden successfully, however, you do need to understand how these natural processes work, since you can thereby use nature's benevolent forces and minimize the damage caused by pests and diseases, without resorting to chemical back-up. The key is to understand just what is possible. You can readily achieve perfectly reasonable crops of vegetables, for example – but perhaps not the intensive yield that commercial growers get by using pesticides and chemicals, or the kind of perfection that you will see on display at the village show.

LEFT *Harvesting your own crops is one of the greatest delights of gardening. Pumpkins are surprisingly easy to grow, provided they have plenty of sun, rich soil and an adequate supply of water.*

CROPPING AND HARVESTING

If you have spent a great deal of energy growing your own fruit and vegetables, it makes sense to ensure not only that they crop adequately, but also that they are in peak condition when the time comes for you to pick them.

One of the key questions for most gardeners is 'How much soil does each plant need?' The answer is that each needs roughly as much space underground as its leaves take up above ground, when fully grown. To some extent you can manipulate the size of the plant by the space you allow its roots. This is true both of container-grown shrubs and of vegetables on the allotment. If you thin out beetroot seedlings so that they are, say, 2cm (1in) apart, you will end up with very small beetroot, no matter how long they grow. If you plant them 4cm (1½in) apart, you will get beetroot roughly 4cm (1½in) in diameter; space them 10cm (4in) apart and you will get much larger beetroot. If, however, you plant your *rows* of beetroot fairly far apart, the beetroot will grow reasonably large, despite the narrowness of the spacing between each one, because it is the distance in all directions from their nearest neighbours that affects their growth.

If space is at a premium, there are ways in which you can utilize the times at which different plants mature to grow twice the number of plants on the available land. Called intercropping, this system is used a great deal in the tropics, where cultivated ground is in short supply. If you want to intercrop, you have to know when your plants will mature. Take carrots and parsnips, for example. You sow them both at the same time, but the carrots mature before the parsnips have reached their full growth, which they go on to do after the carrots have been

RIPENING AND HARVESTING

Not only do you need to look after the plants in your garden, you also need to harvest them with care. Some crops are much more vulnerable than others to damage. Apples such as the Bramley apple and pears, for example, bruise easily, which makes them liable to rot and mould setting in. Strawberries also bruise easily if not handled gently, as do raspberries.

Commercial growers have for some time been heavily engaged in research into how different fruits ripen, because it is in their interests to present the food to the supermarket in the best condition.

Surprisingly perhaps, apples ripen from the inside out. The speed of ripening is linked to the amount of ethylene gas produced by the fruit. As the gas increases, so the fruit sweetens, as the starches in the fruit change to sugars. This change is generated by the pips, which produce hormones that stimulate the outer cells to produce the ethylene that causes the change. Tomatoes are usually picked half-ripe, then graded and packed in boxes, as the ethylene gas given off by the fruit speeds up ripening, especially in an enclosed area such as a tomato tray.

harvested. With this system, you do lose something in crop size, but you more than make up for it by the fact that you have grown two crops on a piece of land that would otherwise have produced only the one crop. Obviously this makes good commercial sense.

Another area in which gardeners are always trying to get the maximum yield in the minimum space is fruit growing. Research undertaken in recent years has produced a wide range of interesting new possibilities for fruit growers, including the introduction of the family tree, in which two or more types of apple are grafted on to one rootstock. You can therefore have, for example, Cox's Orange Pippins sharing a tree with Bramley cooking apples. One advantage of advances in modern grafting techniques (see also page 74) is that they offer great benefits to the town gardener, who simply does not have the space for an old-fashioned orchard, where it was less important if the trees did not all produce their maximum yield. Although many people love the flavour of the Cox's Orange Pippin, it does not set fruit easily, because it has a relatively short period in which the flowers can be fertilized, unlike the heavier-cropping, but less tasty, Golden Delicious. A sport has now been selected and bred that is self-fertile, making the trees less reliant on insect pollination being carried out in a short space of time.

Cordon apple trees, which crop heavily on a very slender tree, are another example of improvements that have been brought about for small-scale gardening. The 'Ballérina' tree, introduced by a Canadian grower from a MacIntosh apple in his orchard, has been extremely successful, producing as it does a heavy crop of apples from a very small amount of tree space.

CROP FAILURE

Despite all your best efforts, crops do occasionally fail, for a variety of reasons. The main ones are either mineral deficiency in the soil or the plant falling prey to pests and diseases. Plants extract different minerals from the soil according to their needs – plants setting a lot of fruit require more potash than most, those being cropped for their leaves require more nitrogen, and so on. Growing the same plant in the same place for several seasons will almost certainly deprive the soil of essential minerals, which is why, since medieval times, farmers have used a system called crop rotation, which helps to prevent this from occurring. Any vegetable plot, with its intensive growth of certain crops, must be organized so that the groups of plants that extract particular minerals from the soil are grown in a different place each year (see plan below).

It is almost always the case that plants that are weak fall prey to disease, but rather than reaching for chemicals from the medicine cupboard, it pays to think a little more carefully about the nutrients that

THE THREE-YEAR CROP ROTATION PLAN

A three-year rotation scheme is suitable for most vegetable gardens. Divide the crops you wish to grow into three groups. Every year, move each group to the next plot, so that two years elapse before any crop returns to its original site. This cuts down the risk of soil-borne disease affecting it.

	A	B	C
Year 1	Peas Beans Onions, leeks Shallots, garlic Lettuces Spinach Spinach beet Celery, celeriac Tomatoes	Cabbages Cauliflowers Broccoli Brussels sprouts Kale Kohlrabi Chinese cabbage Swedes Radishes Turnips	Potatoes Carrots Beetroot Parsnips Salsify Scorzonera Chicory
Year 2	B	C	A
Year 3	C	A	B

you are providing the plant with in the first place. Today people are well aware of the dangers caused by a build-up of chemicals, and also of their effects on both humans and the environment in general. Increasing experimentation has therefore taken place recently into environmentally friendly ways of controlling pests and diseases. Although biological controls do not always offer 100 per cent protection, they frequently reduce the quantity of chemicals needed.

It has been suggested for some time that to reduce the risk of carrot fly, you should grow *Tagetes* marigolds as an intercrop among the carrots. The marigold flowers are a valuable source of pollen and nectar, which attract hover flies, and the larvae of hover flies are notorious predators on a variety of pests that destroy crops. But tests by scientists at Wellesbourne Experimental Station in Warwickshire have so far provided no evidence that interplanting with marigolds actually reduces carrot-fly attacks, although it obviously has an overall beneficial effect, because it provides food for the hover-fly larvae.

The other problem that gardeners face is that certain plants are more prone to attack by particular diseases or insects than others. By and large those with soft, large leaves present the greatest problem, because their leaves offer easily accessible food to the largest number of insects. Take the aubergine, for instance, which has a very large, soft, fleshy leaf that is much appreciated by pests. Aubergines are therefore likely to suffer from aphids, thrips, whitefly, spider mites, leaf miners and leaf hoppers. If you can name it, you will probably find it on the aubergine.

As a result, aubergines – which have to be grown under glass in Britain's climate – have been used to test a new pest-control system called integrated pest management, which encompasses biological control together with parasites, predators and pathogens (disease-causing agents), as growers try to find ways to combat pests and diseases without resorting to chemicals. Glasshouses, like Van Heynigen's nursery in Sussex, where a massive crop of peppers is grown on an area equivalent in size to five football pitches, make an ideal location in which to test some of the latest forms of biological control. With over 21kg (46lb) of peppers for every square metre (1.2sq yd) in the glasshouse, the crop is a sitting target for pests of all descriptions. Various predatory insects – over 30 million predatory mites and countless thousands of predatory midges and wasps – have been deliberately introduced, in order to combat the pests that prey on this particular crop. Unfortunately there is not a predator for every pest, and the peppers are also prone to attacks by leaf hoppers, which can, so far, only be controlled by spray; but one spray a year does the job, so that at least the crop is more organically grown than usual.

Aphids are among the most common garden pests and regularly attack many forms of plant. The most efficient predator of aphids is

FUNGICIDES AND PESTICIDES

The following chemicals, used for treating a variety of pests and diseases, are less environmentally damaging than most. Even so, great care should be taken when storing and using them. Keep anything poisonous under lock and key; make sure that all chemicals are adequately labelled; avoid spraying on a windy day; wash out the sprayer after use; and do not spray on open flowers or during the daytime, to prevent any harm to bees.

Insecticidal Soap This can be sprayed directly on to aphids, whitefly, red spider mites, scale insects and mealy bugs. It lasts for one day only, as does the traditional soft soap, which works in the same way.

Quassia This comes from the bark of a tree, *Picrasma quassiodes*. The spray is effective in controlling aphids, caterpillars, sawfly and leaf miners.

Nicotine Although this is a permitted organic pesticide, the solution can be fatal if drunk neat, so great care should be taken in storing it. Committed organic gardeners make their own nicotine solution by soaking cigarette butts in water, but you have to be extremely dedicated to contemplate such a step. Spray the solution carefully.

Copper Sulphate Available in the form of Bordeaux mixture (in combination with slaked lime) and Burgundy mixture (in combination with washing soda), this is effective in treating mildews and blights.

Pyrethrum Derived from *Chrysanthemum coccineum*, this is effective against most insects, including aphids, but it will also kill off predatory insects, so try to spray it directly on the pests themselves. It is harmless to animals.

the hover fly – the larvae of one species of hover fly (*Syrphus balteatus*) being able to consume an astonishing 600 aphids before it matures.

Hover flies feed only on certain plants. Unlike bees and butterflies, they have relatively short probosces and need flowers with an easy means of access. One of the best of these is *Convolvulus tricolor*, and if you sow these in your vegetable patch in late spring, the flowers will be ready to provide food for the hover flies by midsummer.

Among other predators that are useful to the gardener are ladybirds, which also feed on aphids, lacewings, ground beetles, spiders and centipedes. Hedgehogs are well worth encouraging, since they are a major predator of slugs and snails, which wreak havoc in gardens, feeding on any tender young shoots and leaves that take their fancy (as anyone who tries to grow hostas knows to his cost). Where hedgehogs are in short supply, rather than use slug pellets – which poison the slugs, and indirectly any animals and birds that feed on them – it is just as effective to sink a yoghurt pot of beer into the ground close to the plants that you are trying to protect. The snails and slugs will be attracted by the sweetness and will drown in the beer.

Birds, although likely to do a certain amount of damage themselves, are also useful predators of a whole range of insects. It is probably better to encourage rather than deter them, but you will have to take measures to protect any crops that are particularly vulnerable to birds. Fruit will have to be carefully netted, as will young seedlings. Although some people believe in lacing a network of black cotton over crocuses (which are particularly vulnerable), the idea seems less than satisfactory if, as a friend once did, you have ever seen a bird swinging upside-down in a tree, caught by a piece of dangling thread that had wound itself round its foot and had caught on a branch. (The bird in question – a sparrow – was actually rescued!)

MINERAL DEFICIENCIES

By and large, soil to which well-rotted compost has been added should be rich enough in minerals for the plants grown in it to be free of problems. However, deficiencies do occur and the most commonly found ones are listed below.

Magnesium deficiency often affects tomatoes and lettuces, whose lower leaves (in the case of tomatoes) or outside leaves (in the case of lettuces) go brown and fall off. A quick remedy is 28g (1oz) of magnesium sulphate dissolved in 9 litres (2 gallons) of water and sprayed on to the leaves. The long-term solution is to add more lime to the soil.

Calcium deficiency also often affects tomatoes. It manifests itself in brown patches on the fruit at the blossom end, and the blossom sometimes withers and dies before the fruit is set. Again, liming is the answer. Potatoes that lack calcium will have lots of tubers, but small ones.

Potassium deficiency often occurs on sandy soils, where the potassium leaches out rapidly. Where there is a potassium shortage, the leaves of gooseberries, broad beans, potatoes and tomatoes tend to look scorched. Apply liquid comfrey manure (see below).

Phosphorus deficiency is common on acid soils. Symptoms include purple colouring and streaks on the leaves of carrots, lettuces, cabbages and tomatoes. Apply lots of bonemeal to the soil.

Iron and manganese deficiencies tend to occur in soils that are either naturally very chalky or that have been too enthusiastically limed. The symptoms are very pale green leaves; where iron is in short supply, it is the youngest leaves that lose colour first. One solution is to apply Epsom salts.

LIQUID COMFREY MANURE

If you have a large garden and want to grow vegetables, it makes sense to turn a portion of it over to a comfrey crop, for the purpose of making a good fertilizer – it is excellent for tomatoes, for example. Comfrey (*Symphytum uplandicum*) possesses a rich store of potassium and nitrogen. It grows quickly and its leaves can be cropped four or five times a year. If you add the leaves to a large butt of water, in the ratio of roughly 6kg (14lb) of comfrey to 90 litres (20 gallons) of water, and leave it to rot down for about a month, you will be able to draw off an excellent liquid fertilizer. This contains about three times as much potash, the same quantity of nitrogen and about half the amount of phosphorus that you would find in a traditional tomato fertilizer.

Comfrey is very deep-rooted and has the advantage that you can easily grow it from root cuttings (see page 58), but it is hard to dispose of. When you want to destroy your comfrey crop, use a solution of ammonium sulphate. You will need 0.5kg/1lb of ammonium sulphate to 4.5 litres/1 gallon of water for 9sq m/100 sq ft, sprayed over the bed in spring.

DEALING WITH WEEDS

Weeds cause most gardeners more problems that any other aspect of gardening, and failure to eradicate them is one of the principal causes of crop failure. Since they compete aggressively – for nutrients in the soil, moisture and light – with the plants that you choose to grow, it becomes imperative to remove them before your own plants lose the battle.

It is important to be able to recognize that there are two principal groups of weeds: perennials and annuals. Perennial weeds (as the name implies) last year in, year out, if not removed, since they proliferate by means of either deep roots or creeping stems, as well as seeds. Commonly found perennial weeds include bindweed, dock, ground elder, couch grass and creeping thistle (see right). Depending on your soil and which part of the country you live in, one or more of these will probably predominate in your garden.

When you establish a garden on new ground, or take over a neglected garden, your first efforts have to be directed at clearing the ground of perennial weeds. You can either systematically dig them all up and manually remove them – making sure that you burn them, rather than throwing them on the compost heap, where they will simply re-sprout – or you can use chemical weedkillers, such as glyphosate, after which you will have to leave the ground for a period of time before it is safe to grow plants on it. Alternatively, you can cover the ground with black plastic (with a layer of bark chippings on top to make it less unsightly), which will effectively prevent the weeds from re-sprouting by ensuring that they are unable to photosynthesize (see page 37). Other mulches, such as straw, will help to suppress weeds, but will not do so completely. With black plastic, it will take a couple of years before the weed root finally rots down, if unable to photosynthesize.

Annual weeds, although they last no longer than a season, germinate, flower and seed with alarming rapidity. The commonest annual weeds are chickweed (which is actually very nutritious and can be grown as a crop), groundsel, shepherd's-purse and annual meadow grass. The best method of removing them is to pull them up by hand or hoe them. Whichever method you choose, the most important point to bear in mind is that you should remove them before they seed, since the proverbial 'one year's seedling, seven years' weeding' is certainly not just an old wives' tale. Provided they have not seeded, annual weeds may usefully be put on the compost heap, as they are rich in minerals and nutrients.

PERENNIAL WEEDS TO REMOVE FROM THE GARDEN

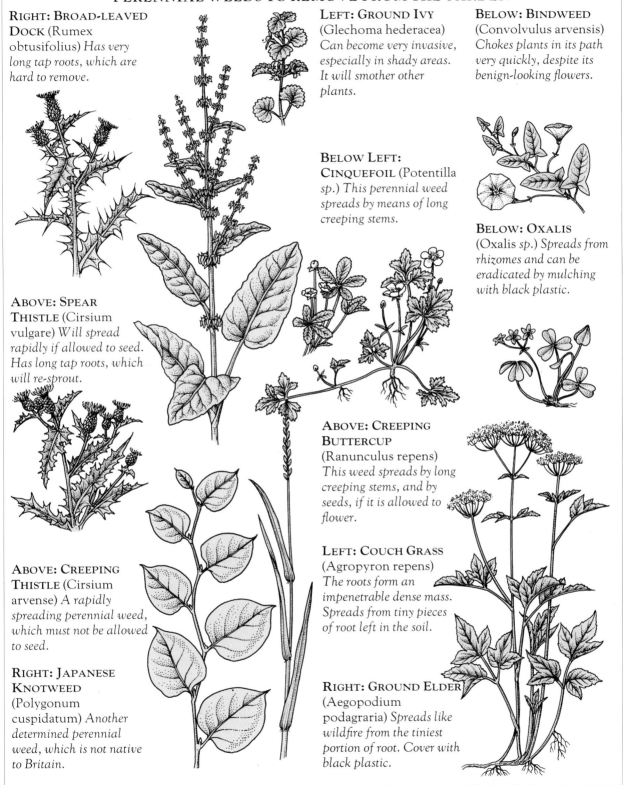

RIGHT: BROAD-LEAVED DOCK (Rumex obtusifolius) *Has very long tap roots, which are hard to remove.*

LEFT: GROUND IVY (Glechoma hederacea) *Can become very invasive, especially in shady areas. It will smother other plants.*

BELOW: BINDWEED (Convolvulus arvensis) *Chokes plants in its path very quickly, despite its benign-looking flowers.*

BELOW LEFT: CINQUEFOIL (Potentilla sp.) *This perennial weed spreads by means of long creeping stems.*

BELOW: OXALIS (Oxalis sp.) *Spreads from rhizomes and can be eradicated by mulching with black plastic.*

ABOVE: SPEAR THISTLE (Cirsium vulgare) *Will spread rapidly if allowed to seed. Has long tap roots, which will re-sprout.*

ABOVE: CREEPING BUTTERCUP (Ranunculus repens) *This weed spreads by long creeping stems, and by seeds, if it is allowed to flower.*

ABOVE: CREEPING THISTLE (Cirsium arvense) *A rapidly spreading perennial weed, which must not be allowed to seed.*

LEFT: COUCH GRASS (Agropyron repens) *The roots form an impenetrable dense mass. Spreads from tiny pieces of root left in the soil.*

RIGHT: JAPANESE KNOTWEED (Polygonum cuspidatum) *Another determined perennial weed, which is not native to Britain.*

RIGHT: GROUND ELDER (Aegopodium podagraria) *Spreads like wildfire from the tiniest portion of root. Cover with black plastic.*

GLOSSARY

ABSCISSION LAYER A layer of cells at the base of a leaf stem, where the leaf breaks away from the main stem.

ACID SOIL Soil that has a pH value of less than seven.

ADVENTITIOUS Arising in places where growth is not normally expected to occur (e.g. when adventitious roots are formed from stems).

ALKALINE SOIL Soil that has a pH value of more than seven.

ALLELOPATH A plant that releases chemicals which prevent the growth of other plants nearby.

ANNUAL A plant that completes its life-cycle in a single growing season.

APICAL BUD The topmost bud on a stem.

APICAL DOMINANCE The ability of the apical bud to inhibit the growth of lateral buds.

AUXIN A naturally occurring chemical that controls plant growth.

BIENNIAL A plant that requires two growing seasons to complete its life-cycle.

BULB A stem base surrounded by swollen food-storage leaves.

CALLUS Cork-like tissue produced by woody plants to cover wounds.

CAMBIUM A layer of cells in the stem of a plant which grow laterally and are the means by which woody plants increase in diameter.

CHLOROPHYLL Green pigment found in plant leaves.

CONTRACTILE ROOT A thickened root that serves to pull bulbs, corms or rhizomes deeper into the soil.

COPPICING The practice of cutting down trees and shrubs to base level to produce new vigorous growth.

CORDON A plant pruned to a single main stem.

CORM A swollen underground stem in which food is stored.

COTYLEDON A single embryonic leaf in seed-bearing plants (a so-called seed leaf).

CROWN The part of a herbaceous plant where roots and stems join, and from which new shoots grow.

CULTIVAR (cv.) A cultivated variety of a plant, usually propagated by horticulturists.

CUTTING Part of a plant used for the purpose of creating a new plant (i.e. stem cutting, root cutting, tip cutting, etc.).

DICOTYLEDON A flowering plant that has two 'seed leaves' in the seedling.

DIVISION The technique of increasing plants by dividing them into pieces, each with a root system and one or more buds.

DORMANCY A state of reduced cellular activity in the plant.

EPIDERMIS The outer layer of plant cells.

EPIPHYTE A plant that uses another plant as a form of structural support.

ESPALIER A tree trained with a single main stem and evenly spaced, laterally trained branches on either side.

FAN A tree trained with a central main stem and its branches at an angle, to resemble a fan shape.

FIBROUS ROOT A thin, branching root near the soil surface.

GENUS A category of plant classification in which related species are grouped.

GERMINATION The start into growth of a seed, spore or pollen grain.

GLAUCOUS Smooth and waxy, applied to leaves.

GRAFTING The technique of creating a union between two or more plants.

HERBACEOUS A plant that is soft and green, without woody tissue.

HYBRID The offspring of two closely related species.

HYPOCOTYL The part of an embryo plant between the cotyledon and the root tip.

INTERCROP A crop grown with other crops, but which matures at a different rate.

LAYERING A method of propagation in which adventitious shoots are encouraged to grow on the stem of the plant while it is still attached to its parent.

LOAM A rich soil consisting of a mixture of sand, clay and decaying organic material.

MERISTEM An area of the plant, usually a shoot or root, where cells actively divide.

MID-RIB The thick central vein of a leaf.

MONOCOTYLEDON A flowering plant that has only one leaf in the seedling (e.g. a leek).

MULCH Any organic or inorganic material applied to the surface of the soil to suppress weeds, conserve moisture and improve soil structure.

MYCORRHIZAE Soil fungi that live in beneficial association with plants.

PERENNIAL A woody or herbaceous plant that continues its growth for at least three years.

PETIOLE The stalk of a leaf.

PHLOEM The food-conducting vessel in a plant.

PHOTOSYNTHESIS The process by which light is absorbed to form food for the plant.

PLEACHING The training of plants by bending and interlacing their shoots.

PODZOL An acidic soil characteristic of coniferous forest regions, with a greyish-white colour in its upper leached layers.

POTENTIAL OF HYDROGEN (pH) A measure of acidity or alkalinity.

RADICLE An embryonic root (root tip).

REMONTANT Blooming more than once in a growing season.

RHIZOME A horizontal underground stem.

ROOTSTOCK A plant used to provide the root system for a grafted plant.

SCION The part of the plant inserted into a rootstock during grafting.

SESSILE Used to describe a leaf that has no stalk (i.e. the blade is attached directly to the stem).

SPECIES (sp.) A group of plants with closely related characteristics.

SPORT A spontaneous or induced genetic change in a plant.

STAMEN The male part of a flower.

STANDARD A tree with a clear length of stem below the branches, which usually start about 2m (6ft) above the soil.

STIGMA The part of the flower that receives the pollen.

STOLON A horizontally spreading stem, which roots at its tip.

STOMATA Pores in the epidermis of plant leaves.

SYMBIOSIS The beneficial relationship between two different organisms.

TAP ROOT A deep root with few branches, used to store food.

TESTA The seed coat or hard, protective outer layer of a seed.

TOPIARY The art of clipping evergreen trees or bushes into artificial decorative shapes.

TOPSOIL The uppermost, highly fertile layer of soil.

TRANSPIRATION The loss of water by evaporation from the leaves and stems of plants.

TUBER The swollen part of a root or stem, used for food storage.

VARIEGATION The irregular coloured pattern on a leaf.

VARIETY A naturally occurring variant of a plant, but often used to refer to cultivars as well.

WOODY Hardy perennial growth.

XYLEM The water-conducting vessel in a plant.

FURTHER READING

Botany for Gardeners by Brian Capon (Timber Press, 1990).

The Concise British Flora in Colour by W. Keble Martin (Ebury Press, 1976).

The Damp Garden by Beth Chatto (J.M. Dent, 1982).

The Dry Garden by Beth Chatto (J.M. Dent, 1978).

The Gardener's Encyclopaedia to Plants & Flowers, edited by Christopher Brickell (Dorling Kindersley, 1990).

The Gardener's Practical Botany by John Tampion (David & Charles, 1972).

Gardening on Clay & Lime by Margery Fish (David & Charles, 1970).

Guide to Practical Gardening, edited by Alan Paterson (Reader's Digest, 1984).

Hillier's Manual of Trees & Shrubs (David & Charles, 1993).

How Does Your Garden Grow? by Peter Hillman (Croom Helm, 1985).

Intermediate Botany by L.J.F. Brimble (Macmillan, 1980).

The Living Garden by E.J. Salisbury (Bell, 1935).

The Low Maintenance Garden by Graham Rose (France Lincoln/Windward, 1983).

Making the Most of Clematis by Raymond J. Evison (Flora Print, 1979).

The Penguin Book of Basic Gardening by Alan Gemmell (Penguin, 1975).

The Practical Gardening Encyclopaedia by Roy Hay (Ward Lock, 1977).

The RHS Book of Plant Propagation by Philip McMillan Browse (Mitchell Beazley, 1979).

The RHS Encyclopaedia of Gardening, edited by Christopher Brickell (Dorling Kindersley, 1992).

The Self-Sufficient Gardener by John Seymour (Dorling Kindersley, 1978).

Successful Organic Gardening by Geoff Hamilton (Dorling Kindersley, 1987).

INDEX

Page references in *italic* refer to illustration captions. * denotes a list of plants.

acid rain 20
acid soils 27–30*
adaptation, plant 85–91
alkaline soils 27; *see also* chalky soils; limey soils
alkaloids 91
Allard, H.A. 116
allelopaths 50
Allium neapolitanum 93
apical meristem 48, *127*
Aspidistra sp. 117
auxins 115, 129

bamboos
    root pruning *55*
bark, ornamental 76*, *76–7*, 131
beech
    coppicing *132*
    seedlings *101*
bluebells 9, *65*
bog gardens 23–4
broad beans
    germination *100*
Brown, 'Capability' 13
buds, apical 127–30
bulbs 60–1, 67
Burren, Ireland 27, *126*
bushes
    fruit trees *142*
    fuchsias *130*
Byron Down Nature Reserve, Kent 30

cacti *4*, 47–8, 86, 89
Californian poppy (*Romneya coulteri*) *56*
callus 74, 78
cambium 74
camouflage 91
Canadian pondweed (*Elodea crispa*) 67
chalk downland *17*, 18
chalky soils 30–1
Chatsworth, Derbyshire *136*
Chatto, Beth 26
chemicals *see* fertilizers; pesticides

cherry (*Prunus serrula*) 76
Chinese lantern tree (*Crinodendrum hookerianum*) 29
chlorophyll 83
chromosomes 127–8
chrysanthemums 117, 128–30
clamps *63*
clay soils *19*, 26*
Clematis 'Niobe' *121*
climbers 12
colour
    autumn 82–4*
    winter 131
comfrey (*Symphytum uplandicum*) 153
competition, plant 6
compost 39–41, 147
compost bins 39, *41*
composts, seed 110
coniferous forest 32, *33*
container growing 31
containers, seed-sowing 108–11
coppicing *131*, 131–2, *132*
cordon fruit trees *142*, 143
corms 62
cowslips 9, *12*

damp ground 24*; *see also* drainage
dandelion seeds *105*
Darwin, Charles 43, 122, 123
day-length *see* photoperiodism
dead-heading 138
defence mechanisms, plant 89–91
digging 20–1, 42–3
dividing 58–9*
dogwoods (*Cornus* sp.) *131*
dormancy 67, 102–4
    double *104*
drainage 20; *see also* soakaways
drills 107–8
drought 20, 84
dry shady/sunny areas 26*
Dutch elm disease 136
dwarf pyramid fruit trees 142–3

earthworms 12, 20, 34, 43
East Malling Horticultural Research station, Kent 52
epiphytes 18, *45*, 46

espalier fruit trees *141*, *142*, 144–5
evening primroses (*Oenothera* sp.) *113*

fan fruit trees *142*, 144, 145
fashions in gardening 13
Fenlands 18
fertilization 94
fertilizers 35, 36
field daisies 14
field poppy (*Papaver rhoeas*) *104*
Fish, Margery 26
flame nettle (*Coleus*) *81*
flowers
    anatomy 93
    pruning 137–40; *see also under* species
frogs 9
fruit trees
    grafting 149
    pruning 141–2
    shapes *142*
    training 142–5
fruits
    harvesting 148
    ripening 148
fuchsias, standard and bush *130*
fungicides 152

Gardner, W.W. 116
germination 7
giant lily (*Cardiocrinum giganteum*) 61
Gilbert, Henry 13
glass, growing under 118–19*, 151
grafting 74–6, 149
grasses 15*, 26*, 49–51
ground cover 51*
growth, plant 53–4, 127–30
growth hormones *see* auxins
Gunnera manicata 88

Haddon Hall, Derbyshire *133*
hollies 89
horse chestnuts (*Aesculus* sp.) 83, 84
house plants 91, 117
    propagation 80

indicator species 27
insectivorous plants 122
insects
    pollinating 93, 95*

predatory 151
intercropping 148, 151
iris rhizomes 62
    division 59
ivies 46
    (*Hedera colchica* 'Dentata variegata') 69

Jekyll, Gertrude 13

Kalanchoe 81
Kew Gardens 52, 122

Lake District 20
lawns 49–51
    mowing and growth 49, 50
Laws, John 13
layering 79*
leaf cuttings 80–1*
leaves 65–6
    adaptations 85–7
    arrangements and shapes 68–9, 86
    fall 83
    movements 116
    pigments 82
    stomata 69–70
    variegated 87–8*, 89
    vein patterns 86
light 114–17
lily bulbs 60
lime and liming 20, 27–8
limey soils 30*
Linnaeus, Carolus 115
loam *19*
Lobelia keniensis 65
Loudon, J.C. 115

manures, liquid 153
Marden Meadow, Kent 14
marram grass (*Ammophila arenaria*) *51*
marrows
    germination *101*
Mount Usher Gardens, Ireland 29
mulches 38, 154
    bark chippings 40
    black plastic 12, 37, 39, 40, 63, 154

nitrogen (N) 35
nitrogen cycle 36
no-dig system 43
nutrients 35; *see also* fertilizers

orange pips 100

organic gardening 12, 13, 147
oxeye daisies *12, 14*

palm fronds 85
paper-bark maple (*Acer griseum*) 76
parsley
growing from seed 102
Paxton, Joseph 118
pest control, biological 151–2
pesticides 11–12, 152
pH tests *see* soil testing
phosphate (P) 35
photoperiodism 116
photosynthesis 66–7, 101
plastic, black 12, 37, 39, *40*, 63, 154
pleaching 135, *136*
poinsettia (*Euphorbia pulcherrima*) 117
poisonous plants 91*
pollarding *131*, 131–2
pollination 93–5
pollution 20
ponds 15
potagers 149
potash (K) 35
potatoes
planting *63*
potatoes, seed
chitting 111
propagation *see* dividing; layering; leaf cuttings; root cuttings; stem cuttings
propagators 110
pruning 127, 131–2, 137–45; *see also* root pruning
pumpkins *147*

raised beds *21, 31*
Repton, Humphry 13
rhizomes 51, 59, 62
Robinson, William 13
root-bound plants *55*
root cuttings 56*, 58

root pruning 54–5
roots
adventitious 58, 78, 120
aerial *45, 46*
buttress *45,* 46–7
fibrous 47–8, *49,* 58–9
functions 46
gravitational response 115
growth 48
hairs 34, 48
tap 47–8
tree 52–5
Rosa 'Matangi *140*
roses
pruning 138–40
types 139*
Rothamstead experimental station, Hertfordshire 13
runner beans
supports *121*

sandy soils 19
Sang Dragon tree (*Pterocarpus indica*) 45
sedums *73*
seedbeds 43, 106
seeds 96
anatomy 96
chilling 104
dispersal 96–8
germination 99–101, 106
saving and storage 103
sowing 105–11
stratification 102–3
Sequoia giganteum 72
shady areas *25,* 26*, 117
shaping, plant 125–45
silt 19
snake-bark maple (*Acer grosseri*) 76
snake's head fritillaries 14
Snowdonia, Wales 27
soakaways *22*
soil
bacteria 21, 50
compaction 21–2
creation 32–3
fungi 50

improvement 19–22
influence of geology 18
micro-organisms 34
nutrient cycling 34–6
nutrient deficiencies 36–7, 153
preparation *see* seedbeds
structure 19–22
waterlogging 22
see also under soil types
soil samples
podzol and garden soil *32,* 32–3
soil testing 19, 27, 29
sowing seeds 105–11
spacing, plant 148
squirting cucumber (*Ecballium elaterium*) 97
standards
fruit trees *142*
fuchsias *130*
stem cuttings 78–9*
stems 74–7
stimuli, plant 114–17, 122–3
stinging nettle (*Urtica dioica*) 90
storage
root vegetables 63
seeds 103
suckers 59
sun rose (*Cistus × purpureus*) *25*
sundial plants 115*
sunflowers (*Helianthus* sp.) *4,* 113
supports 120–1
swedes
clamping *63*
symbiosis 50

tannins 90
Teesdale 18, 27
Thymus praecox articus 17
Tillandsia ionantha 'Scaposa' *45*
topiary 133–5
Tradescant, John 118

transpiration 71–3
trees 52
moving *54*
outlines *126*
planting 54
pruning 131–2
roots 52–5
see also fruit trees *and under species*
tubers 62
root 63
tulip bulbs 60

vegetables
crop rotation 150
seed saving 103*
storage 63
see also drills *and under names of vegetables*
vegetables, root 63*
Venus flytrap (*Dionaea muscipula*) 123

Wakehurst Place, Sussex 136
watering 49, 71
in sunshine 70
waterlogged soils 22; *see also* drainage
weather 106
weed control 154–5; *see also* ground cover; mulches
weeds 42, *155*
Wellesbourne Experimental Station, Warwickshire 151
Whin Sill 27
wild-flower meadows 14–15*
willows
pollarding *131*
wilted plants 71
Wisley, Surrey
water gardens *24*
worms *see* earthworms

yarrows *14*

ACKNOWLEDGEMENTS

I would like to thank Dr Mark Lyne of Writtle College and Flashback Television for their advice, and Frances Currie for producing transcripts of the television programmes. Brian Capon's book *Botany for Gardeners* was an invaluable source of information and a worthwhile book to obtain for anyone wanting to know more about plant biology. I am also very grateful to Mandy Greenfield for her editorial work on the manuscript, and to Nigel Partridge for his design input.

SUSAN BERRY

I would like to thank Neil Cleminson and Taylor Downing of Flashback Television for giving me the opportunity to work on the television series *Plant Life*.

STEVE BRADLEY

The authors and publishers are grateful to the following for permission to reproduce copyright material: Beth Chatto for the lists of plants on p. 26 (taken from the catalogue of her nursery, The Beth Chatto Gardens Ltd, Elmstead Market, Colchester, Essex); John Seymour for symptoms of soil deficiency on p. 37 (taken from *The Self-Sufficient Gardener*, Dorling Kindersley, 1978); Penguin Books for the table of main fertilizers on p. 35 (taken from p. 54 of *The Penguin Book of Basic Gardening* by Alan Gemmell, 1975), copyright © Alan Gemmel, 1975. Reproduced by permission of Penguin Books Ltd.

PICTURE CREDITS

The illustrations are reproduced by kind permission of the following:

Heather Angel: pp. 8, 17, 45, 49, 64, 72, 73, 84, 92, 97, 101, 104, 105, 113, 121, 146
Neil Cleminson: pp. 12, 13, 149
Brian Mathew: pp. 33, 65, 85
Oxford Scientific Films Ltd: pp. 16, 48, 70, 127
Photos Horticultural Picture Library: front and back jackets, pp. 1, 4–5, 9, 25 (both), 40 (both), 44, 50, 51, 57, 69, 76, 77, 90, 109, 112, 119, 123, 124, 128, 129, 132, 133, 136 (top), 140, 149
David Secombe: pp. 53, 61, 81 (left), 88
Harry Smith Horticultural Photographic Collection: pp. 21, 24, 28, 29, 81 (right), 89, 95, 117, 125, 136 (bottom), 144 (right).
Steven Wooster: pp. 141, 144 (left)

Line drawings by Will Giles and Sandra Pond.